KYLIE

FEVER

CARLTON
BOOKS

THIS IS A CARLTON BOOK

Published by Carlton Books Limited 2002
20 Mortimer Street
London W1N 7RD

A CIP catalogue for this book is available from the
British Library.

ISBN 1 84222 889 7

Managing Editor: Lorna Russell
Managing Art Director: Clare Baggaley
Design: Michelle Pickering
Jacket Design: Alison Tutton
Picture Research: Adrian Bentley
Production: Lisa Moore

Printed and bound in Italy

10 9 8 7 6 5 4 3 2 1

CONT

ENTS

INTROD

It's summer 2002 and we're at one of the most eagerly anticipated concerts of the year. Kylie Minogue is in town. It doesn't matter which town: it could be Cardiff, London, Glasgow or Sheffield. Throughout the country every show is a sell-out, her latest album, *Fever*, is the biggest thing she's ever done and

"I think my gold hot

the famously diminutive star has never been bigger. Even across the water in the notoriously difficult to impress US, they've caught on.

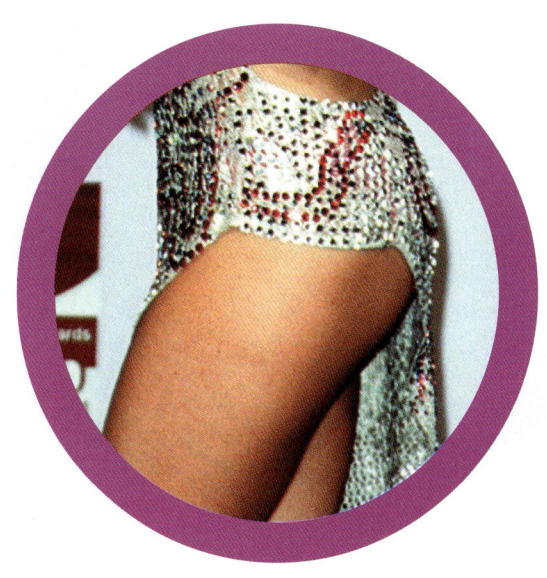

But there's something different in the crowd here in Britain. Look around. Here more than anywhere it's impossible to talk about a typical Kylie Minogue fan.

s stole the show. I don't think I get

White, black, young, old, male, female, gay, straight – she unites the entire country like no other pop star and, scattered among this cross section of the public, you'll find several ecstatic 15-year-olds who have a particular connection with the perfectly formed Australian. See, in Britain, Kylie's story didn't begin with 'Can't Get You Out Of My Head'. It didn't even begin with the previous year's hit 'Spinning Around'.

Here, in these massive arenas, we're talking about a love affair that goes right back to 1987. The self-assured sex-bomb who now stalks the stage is even more special because we remember

noticed at all. Those little hot pants have a

life of their own and they're off and running."

Kylie as Charlene in *Neighbours*. We don't just remember 15 years of fantastic pop singles and affairs with the likes of Jason Donovan and Michael Hutchence. We also remember the dodgy hairstyles, the fashion mistakes, the way she grew up in public, changed her image and then changed it back again, without ever losing the affection of her fans.

That's why in this country there are dozens of girls born in the late 1980s who bear a name that, in the past, was almost unknown outside Australia. It's an aboriginal word meaning boomerang. The name is Kylie: she who always comes back.

IN THE BEGINNING

IN THE BEGINNING

IN THE BEGINNING

ONE

CHAPTER 1

There are two sides to Kylie. On the one hand she's one of the most charismatic, likable stars in the world, but that alone isn't enough to explain the kind of success she's had. There's also a cool-headedness about her, a pragmatism and an inner steel that, for a long time, the general public and the media never saw. For this we can give the credit to her mum and dad, Carol and Ron Minogue.

Carol was born in a
small Welsh town called
Maesteg at the end of World War II.
In 1955, when she was just ten years old,
her parents, Dennis and Millie Jones,
decided to emigrate to Queensland, Australia,
taking their four children Jean, Carol, Suzette
and Noel with them. In Australia Carol
began attending ballet lessons and she
was very soon a talented ballerina who
dreamed of turning professional.

When she was 18 Carol
met and eventually married
fifth-generation Australian Ron
Minogue, a pragmatic accountant who
would later pass a watchful eye over
Kylie's financial affairs. Carol gave up
dancing to raise a family with Ron and on
28 May 1968 their first child, Kylie,
was born at Bethlehem Hospital in
their new home of Melbourne.

At this point in many biographies we'd be reaching for a box of tissues as we began to trawl through the starlet's tear-jerkingly deprived youth. In Kylie's case, however, this doesn't apply. Her childhood was only remarkable for its complete and utter normality. If anything she seems to have had fewer traumas than most people. Ron and Carol are still together and Kylie once said, "I've never heard my parents argue, never ever. I think everyone in the world's parents have got divorced, apart from mine."

Despite her mother's dance background and the fact that several other family members were in show business, Kylie was never the stereotypical child-actress brat. She went to a normal school and did normal things. In the many interviews she's given, the nearest thing we get to childhood misery is a distaste for the Melbourne school system's fondness for vivisection. "I had to cut up sheep's eyeballs," she once groaned squeamishly to style magazine *The Face*. "It was awful. An eyeball, looking at you! It was really hard to cut. It went all over the place. I didn't want anything to do with it!"

Like so many other little girls at the time, Kylie fantasised about being Australian singer/actress Olivia Newton-John. She used to stand in front of the mirror singing 'You're The One That I Want' into a hairbrush, unselfconsciously imagining what it would be like to be Sandy from *Grease*.

Understandably at that age, Kylie was much keener on the glamour of performing than on the reality of learning to play a musical instrument, although to begin with it was fun. At the age of about four, Ron and Carol took her to a "musical rhythm" class near her home in Melbourne, but this involved little more than the children banging sticks together and making as much noise as possible.

Then, when she was still only a very small child, Kylie started learning the violin. She had

So that's where she gets that smile from. *Opposite:* Kylie with her mum Carol, 1989. *Above:* Kylie at the start of her pop career, 1988.

band aids showing her where to play and her tiny fingers struggled to control even the child-sized violin they'd given her. It must have been a relief, at the age of seven, to switch to the piano. Kylie was a natural at music, learning by ear and picking things up quickly, but at such a young age she never had the drive or the patience to stick at anything for long. It was then, perhaps, that she started working on the killer charm that would serve her so well in the music industry.

When Kylie was eight, her proud mum Carol entered her in a local piano competition. As she patiently waited for her turn alongside various child prodigies, the young Kylie could have been forgiven for a serious attack of stage fright. After all, she's the first to admit that she was never all that assiduous about practising her scales.

Not for the last time, however, she was to prove that success is about much more than just technical skill. "Apparently," she told *Metro*, "I walked on stage, turned and gave a big smile to the judges, then proceeded to play 'Run Rabbit Run', gave them another really big smile and promptly walked off with second prize. I just charmed it out of them!"

She was still a long way from considering music as a career, though. Instead she became obsessed by ponies. Every Saturday morning a fresh copy of horse bible *Trading Post* dropped on to her doormat and she used to rush downstairs and pore over every page – even the classified ads. "I could tell you what a secondhand bridle cost," she once admitted to men's magazine *FHM*. "How sad is that?"

As she approached her teens, however, the allure of ponies began to pall. With her trademark determination, Kylie moved on to a new set of interests: pop music and boys. In the early 1980s, heavily made-up so-called New Romantic bands ruled the roost and the first pop idol to make an impression on her was the theatrical ex-punk Adam Ant. "He was so gorgeous. I still kind of shudder at the name," she breathed recently.

The strong-willed teen even tried to bully her younger brother Brandan into liking the same kind of music. He was into kitsch glam-rock bands like Kiss, but at that time Kylie was much more interested in the cooler likes of Siouxsie and the Banshees. Her efforts to convert him came to nothing, though. "He continued to prance about in my mother's thigh-high vinyl high-heeled boots with her make-up on, stars around his eyes, screaming 'Kiss will live forever!' And he wasn't far wrong," she told *FHM*.

Opposite: Kylie's brother Brandon got the Minogue smile, too – shame he didn't get her taste in music, 1993.

> " Brandan continued to prance about in my mother's thigh-high vinyl high-heeled boots with her make-up on, stars around his eyes, screaming 'Kiss will live forever!' And he wasn't far wrong. "

Kylie congratulates
Dannii after her
sister's West End
debut in the
musical *Notre Dame
de Paris*, 2000.

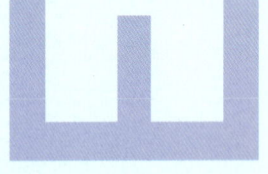

Music wasn't a priority at that time – she much preferred hanging around with her friends at the glamorous meeting point of Melbourne Municipal Baths. It was there, at the age of 13, that she had her first kiss. "I thought he was quite exotic with his crazy, curly black hair," she told *Smash Hits* much later (and probably all her friends at the time).

All the encouragement Ron and Carol had given her to take up music seemed to have come to nothing but they didn't mind. She was happy doing normal, suburban Australian things. However, even before ponies, Adam Ant and wild-haired young Lotharios came into the picture, Kylie had managed to exercise her artistic side. At the age of nine she'd won a support role in *The Sullivans*, one of Australia's

biggest soaps of the time. If she was ever going to be a star, it looked like it would be as an actress rather than as a musician.

Kylie's Aunt Suzette had heard that the producers of *The Sullivans* were looking for talented child actors. She immediately suggested that they take a look at her niece – Dannii. Kylie's sister was by far the more dedicated performer of the two. "And, of course, my mother said, 'Well, can I bring both girls in?'" Kylie remembers. As it turned out, Dannii was too young for the part on offer, a Dutch girl called Carla, so Kylie got the job instead. Although the two sisters have always denied rumours of rivalry between them, this must have been difficult for Dannii to deal with.

However, by no stretch of the imagination was *The Sullivans* a launch pad to success for Kylie. She was supposed to speak in a Dutch accent but at that age she found it hard to avoid slipping back into her Australian twang. "I must have had the worst accent," she groans now. In fact, apart from a small role in a drama called *Skyways* (where a small blond boy called Jason Donovan played her brother), she mostly put her acting career on hold for another five years while she concentrated on school. Instead, it was Dannii who would become a household name. Kylie's younger sister was the star of a highly popular variety show called *Young Talent Time*. She was on TV every week and the tables were turned.

"My sister was the famous one," says Kylie. "She was the one who was recognised in the street." It wasn't until Kylie took a role in children's drama *The Henderson Kids* at the age of 16 that she started taking acting seriously again. "The first interview I had to do for *The Henderson Kids*, I remember saying, 'I don't want you to call me Dannii's sister. Call me Kylie'," she told *Metro*.

It was during the making of *The Henderson Kids* that Kylie first experienced what it was like to be different. The programme already had one blonde girl and the producers felt that having two would be confusing for viewers. They decided that her character, Charlotte Kernow, should be a redhead. "I'll never forget," she told *Smash Hits*. "I went to school and my hair was just bright red, especially in the sunlight because it had just been done, and as you can imagine, bright red dye onto blonde hair was pretty shocking. I had to tell everyone that I hadn't done it out of my own free will, I had to have it done. I was so embarrassed."

However, despite her embarrassment, the role got her hooked on acting. She got to go away with a big group of other kids of the same age and they all became good friends. They were given about $10 a day to spend on food and, for the first time, Kylie got to spend the night away from home and away from her family. It was an extremely important experience in her life.

Charlotte Kernow, or Char as the character was known, may not have set the world on fire but she was crucial to Kylie's career. The feisty redhead was a bit of a tomboy. She could easily have been the younger sister of the character who would make Kylie Minogue one of the biggest stars in Britain and in many other parts of the world: Charlene Mitchell of *Neighbours*.

After *The Henderson Kids* Kylie appeared in two other series, *Fame and Misfortune* and *Zoo Family*, but she was still trying to combine her acting career with studying for her high-school diploma. In 1984 she finished school at the age of 16 and she had to make a decision. Should she look for a "proper" job or should she try to make it as an actress?

Above: 1988: Hope that's not Ramsey Street – the wall could collapse at any moment.
Opposite: 1980s Kylie – some tomboy!

NEIGHBOURS

NEIGHBOURS

KYLIE

2

CHAPTER

TWO

Until quite late in her showbiz career, Kylie still assumed that one day she'd have to get a normal job. "I would have made a great secretary," she says, "because I love organising things!" However, she chose to carry on with acting. Like thousands of other wannabe actors, she resigned herself to being out of work and signed on the dole, but she also got herself an agent and soon her decision to pursue acting was justified.

Charlene regrets
letting Madge cut
her hair, 1988.

"I did sign on for the dole when I finished school," Kylie admits. "I wanted to be an actress – that's what you do." However, just a few weeks after she'd finished her exams and before she'd received her first dole cheque, Kylie had already found a major role in a daytime soap.

The year Kylie left school, successful TV executive Reg Watson of Australian production company Grundy was working on a new soap. It was to be called *Neighbours*. In the past he'd been responsible for programmes like *Prisoner Cell Block H*, with strong, dramatic story lines and a powerful cult appeal. When he suggested a soap based around three normal, working-class families living on a suburban street, there was understandable confusion from his bosses.

However, on the strength of his record, they made the programme. It was a complete disaster. Ratings were terrible and broadcasters Channel Seven ditched it after 170 episodes. At that point it looked like it was all over but, unexpectedly, rival broadcaster Channel Ten stepped in and agreed to show the programme if certain changes were made. Grundy went away, brainstormed for a while, and came up with some new ideas. Chief among these was the introduction of new, attractive, youthful characters that a young audience could identify with.

Are they or aren't they? Kylie with *Neighbours* co-star Jason Donovan.

"KYLIE"

"When she got in front of the camera, I looked at the monitor and thought, 'Hang on, we've got something here.' She has an incredible love affair with the camera."

A stream of young talent flowed through Grundy's doors as the desperate producers searched for someone to give the ailing programme a bit of spark. Cue Kylie. The role of feisty, tomboyish mechanic Charlene Mitchell was perfect for her. Although we now think of Kylie as the petite, delicate Absinthe fairy of *Moulin Rouge*, or the cheeky, ultra-feminine star of the 'Can't Get You Out Of My Head' video, you have to remember that she'd already played the proto-Charlene – Charlotte Kernow in *The Henderson Kids*.

Initially, however, Kylie seemed subdued and nervous when she walked into Grundy's studios. "When she came in for the initial audition she was as quiet as a mouse," says *Neighbours* casting director Jan Russ. However, Russ soon realised that Kylie was exactly what the show was looking for. "When she got in front of the camera," says Jan, "I looked at the monitor and thought, 'Hang on, we've got something here.' She has an incredible love affair with the camera." But, even then, nobody had any idea how big *Neighbours* would become. Or how crucial the chemistry between Kylie Minogue and Jason Donovan would be to its success.

The producers had made the right decision by investing in youth. The programme was saved when the BBC picked it up to fill a hole in its daytime programming. The mixture of sunshine, a little light drama and a healthy smattering of chirpy Australians was irresistible. During the school holidays, half the nation's kids got hooked on it and, perhaps in order to avert a truancy crisis when school started again, it was switched to a later time slot. From there it just got bigger and bigger.

The episode where Charlene Mitchell married Scott Robinson (significantly this is always referred to as the episode where Kylie married Jason) was one of the most watched in soap history. Kylie's initial contract of just 12 weeks was extended and then extended again until she ended up staying on Ramsay Street for two and a half years.

In 1987 she became the youngest person ever to receive a Silver Logie (Australia's equivalent of the Bafta) for Most Popular Actress and she was a genuine star. However, despite her success, she wasn't always happy. "I didn't go to college," she said to men's magazine *GQ*. "I went straight into a soap. So all my memories from that era are related to that. Whereas people my age still have friends from college, I have a career. It's sad, really."

The reality of life as a soap actress was very different from the relentless sunshine portrayed on screen. Every morning the soap stars would meet in the green room, smoking, drinking coffee and desperately learning their lines. After work they'd go home, eat and try to learn their script for the next morning before finally falling asleep exhausted.

There were also rumours of discord between the established actors who'd been working in television for years and the new faces brought in as much for their looks as their acting skills. *Neighbours* was by no means as easy as it looked. "I just remember working my butt off for years and very little else. It was tough, speed-learning your lines in about 20 seconds and then going on to the next scene," Kylie stated. In April 1987 she told reporters, "I don't know if I'll be in this business for long, so I have to use what's happening now to my advantage." She said she intended to study fashion "in case I need something to fall back on".

As it turned out, she didn't need anything to fall back on. *Neighbours* became huge and everybody wanted a piece of the action. One British newspaper announced a competition to win a trip to the set. They had a staggering one million entries in just three days. Gossip about the stars' private lives made the front pages and there was constant speculation about the real relationship between Kylie and Jason.

KYLIE

Above: "And the winner of 'Best Supporting Mullet' is …" Kylie and Jason wait anxiously at the Logie Awards, 1988. *Opposite:* Girl-next-door makes the perfect *Neighbour*.

This reached its zenith at 1988's Logies, where Kylie was crowned the most popular TV star Australian television had ever known. She won an unrivalled four awards in one night, including the Gold Logie for Most Popular Television Personality. At the same time Jason picked up the award for Most Popular Actor and *Neighbours* itself won Most Popular Drama Series. Instead of celebrating, however, Kylie returned to her hotel room where she collapsed in tears.

Neighbours was never meant to be this big. It was just fluff, a bit of daytime filler. The actors and actresses often worked 12-hour days and they were expected to have short shelf lives, to be almost as dispensable as the sets. Kylie, Jason and others changed all that. Quite unexpectedly they had become bigger than the show that had made them.

However, tiring of the soap treadmill, Kylie and Jason were both eager to broaden their horizons. In retrospect their decision to launch singing careers seems obvious. Dozens of young soap stars have tried it since with varying degrees of success, but at the time it seemed absurd. Who would buy a record by Charlene Mitchell or Scott Robinson? The answer came sooner than they thought.

BECOMING A
POP STAR

KYLIE

BECOMING A

CHAPTER

3

THREE

BECOMING A POP STAR

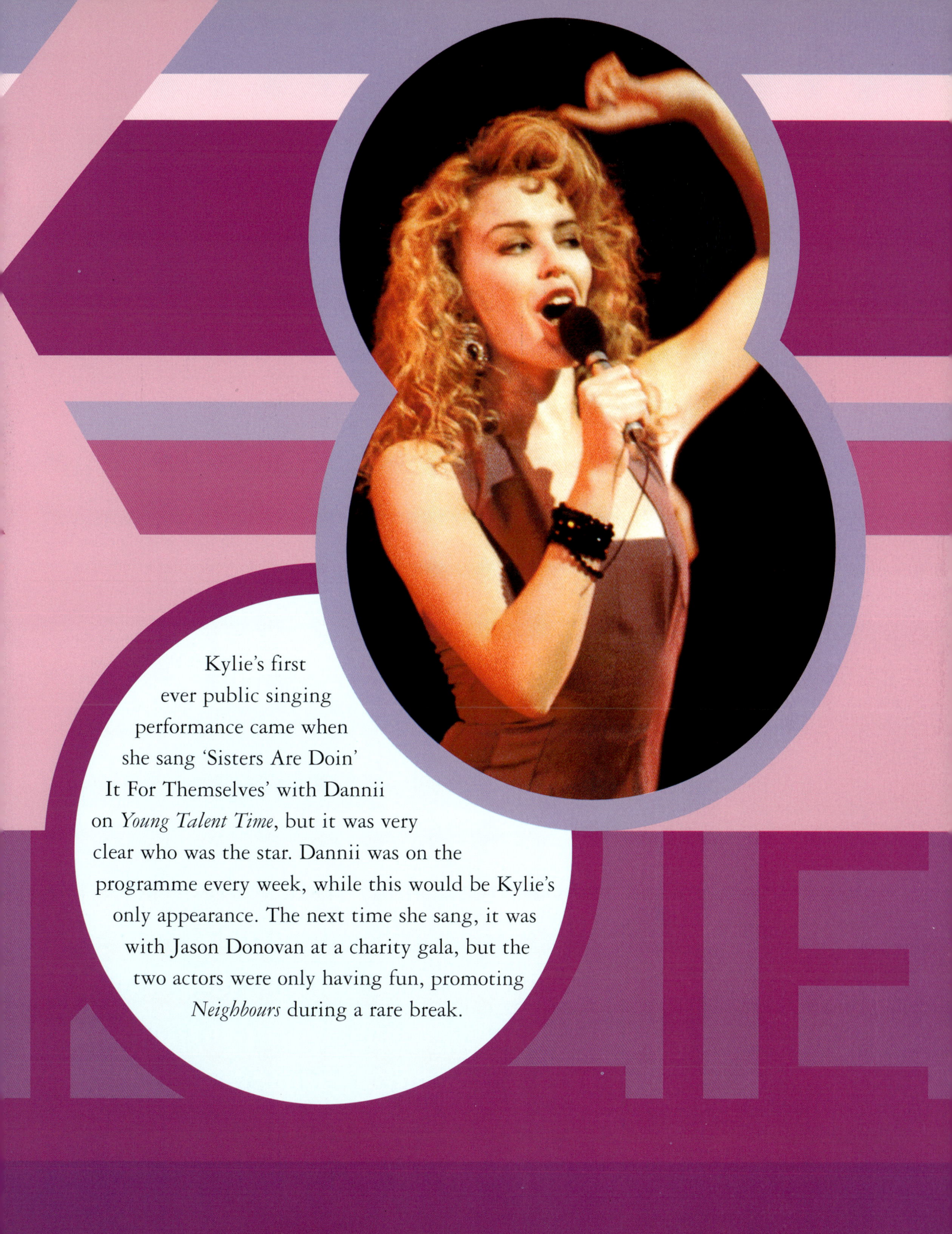

Kylie's first ever public singing performance came when she sang 'Sisters Are Doin' It For Themselves' with Dannii on *Young Talent Time*, but it was very clear who was the star. Dannii was on the programme every week, while this would be Kylie's only appearance. The next time she sang, it was with Jason Donovan at a charity gala, but the two actors were only having fun, promoting *Neighbours* during a rare break.

With *Neighbours* becoming so popular, such promotional activities were becoming more frequent. Towards the end of the year the whole cast appeared at a huge charity benefit at an Australian football club. Some of the actors, including Alan Dale who played Jim Robinson, had formed a sort of house band. At the last minute they asked Kylie if she'd sing the old Little Eva song 'The Locomotion' with them. She agreed and, in the happy-go-lucky spirit of the born performer, she blasted the song out for the arena of delighted *Neighbours* fans.

Outside in the crowd was a producer called Mike Duffy. He was so impressed with Kylie's performance that he immediately suggested she record 'The Locomotion' as a single. With some reservations she accepted. Kylie was never the kind of person who thought that she could instantly master anything she turned her hand to. She worried that her singing voice wasn't strong enough. She also worried that nobody would be interested. However, to everyone's surprise, the resulting record was immediately a huge hit. Eventually it became Australia's biggest-selling single of the 1980s.

Still, Kylie wasn't under any illusions. The career of the average pop star in the 1980s was every bit as fleeting as it is now and, if she wanted to make a new career away from *Neighbours* (and she certainly did), she couldn't just rely on covers. What she needed was somebody who could provide a steady stream of tunes for her to record as quickly as possible so that she could capitalise on her popularity while it lasted. In 1987 there was only one song-writing team that fitted the bill. They were called Stock, Aitken and Waterman.

Pete Waterman was a maverick record producer who'd made his name in the industry as an R&B and Motown fanatic. Mike Stock and Matt Aitken were songwriters whom Pete had roped in to create a phenomenal hit factory. In 1987 they had 31 number ones around the world and sold a staggering 35 million records. And remember, this was before they had Kylie or Jason on board.

When Kylie flew out to London to make a record with the legendary S/A/W, she was just one of many hopeful starlets looking for a break, and she was made aware of this fact very quickly. After a long flight from Australia, she waited expectantly for them to get in touch but heard nothing. Eventually she turned up at their offices and discovered that they'd forgotten all about her and had nothing ready for her to record. "She was in London for three or four days before we even knew she was here," remembered Mike Stock to *Number One* magazine. "Her manager turned up and said, 'Well, we're here!' I didn't even know who she was because I didn't watch *Neighbours* and her manager said, 'We're making a record with you and unless you make it today we're in trouble because we fly back tomorrow.' That was it!"

"Her manager turned up and said, 'Well, we're here!' I didn't even know who she was because I didn't watch *Neighbours* and her manager said, 'We're making a record with you and unless you make it today we're in trouble because we fly back tomorrow.' That was it!"

ESPECIALLY FOR YOU

As legend has it, Mike and Matt then went into a huddle in the back office and within a few minutes they'd written a song for her. The song was called 'I Should Be So Lucky'. According to Mike, "Matt and I were galvanised into action. We wrote it there and then and based it around what we knew about her. We quickly gleaned that she was a soap star and that she was very young and very successful and we thought, 'Bloody hell, we should be so lucky!'"

This story sounds almost too good to be true, but Stock, Aitken and Waterman were known for the exceptional speed of their song writing. They claimed to have written 1980s star Rick Astley's earlier smash 'Never Gonna Give You Up' in just three and a half minutes. The secret of their success was that they worked to a tried-and-tested formula. It was a combination of catchy, instantly memorable tunes and a charismatic star who would do the tunes justice and look good on TV.

Opposite: Kylie and Jason sing 'Especially For You', 1988.
Above: Kylie, ready for the SAW treatment in 1988.

Right: PunkKylie?
Opposite: **Kylie in tight shorts. Now there's an idea.**

"It was all done very quickly," remembers Pete Waterman, "and then at our Christmas party six weeks later, I was sitting down after dinner and the disco was going and this track came on and I ran over to the DJ and said 'What's that!? It's fantastic!' He said, 'It's Kylie Minogue, "I Should Be So Lucky".' And I went over to Mike and said 'That's gonna be a smash!'"

However, even then the record industry wasn't interested. Despite S/A/W's incredible track record, every company Pete Waterman approached turned him down flat. Undeterred, he decided to set up his own company, PWL, and Kylie's 'I Should Be So Lucky' would be the first major single on it. In a recent documentary on Radio One, Pete claimed that he was inspired by the explosion of punk rock a few years before.

"Without punk there would be no Kylie because she was perfect punk," he said. "That was the most punk act I've ever done … Every A&R guy said, 'You'll never sell a soap star.' Now, it doesn't look punk, but we stuck our fingers up and said 'F**k it' and put the record out and sold a million copies. The attitude we adopted was: 'We'll do it ourselves.' The

“ I was sitting down after dinner and the disco was going and this track came on and I ran over to the DJ and said 'What's that!? It's fantastic!' He said, 'It's Kylie Minogue, "I Should Be So Lucky".' And I went over to Mike and said 'That's gonna be a smash!' ”

physical effort of putting that record out was as outrageous as Malcolm McLaren putting his first record out. You just didn't see it like that."

No one saw it like that but, in one respect, Pete Waterman is right. Kylie's pop career didn't just roll off the record industry production line. These days talent spotters, the A&R guys, are adept at pulling people off the TV and into the recording studio, but in 1987 things didn't work that way. The biggest stars were groups like the Pet Shop Boys or dedicated, ambitious singers like the all-powerful Madonna.

As Pete had promised, the record was a smash. In January 1988 'I Should Be So Lucky' went to number one in the British pop charts and it remained in the charts for 16 weeks. The next obvious step was to start recording an album. By now, Stock, Aitken and Waterman had developed a healthy respect for the affection Kylie commanded among her army of *Neighbours* fans and they knew it would be a huge success. "Kylie could have come in and burped into the mike and it would have been a hit," they once modestly said.

As Pete Waterman told the Australian version of *Smash Hits* at the time: "In Australia you've got no idea how the kids in England adore her. She is enormous over there. *Neighbours* has become an institution in England because none of the English shows can compare to it – it's the kids' soap opera."

Inevitably, Pete Waterman started out by re-doing the only song she'd done before falling into his clutches: 'The Locomotion'. "We re-did it for Kylie's album because I didn't like the Australian version," he told *Smash Hits*. "It's my favourite song of all time and I don't think it did Kylie any justice. They got the chords wrong for a start, and the male voices on it are quite obnoxious. We've made it more like the original – and we've got the chords right."

CHAPTER THREE

Below and opposite:
By the end of the
year (1988) Kylie
was getting used
to the cameras.

"Kylie could have come in and burped into the mike and it would have been a hit.

The rest of her debut album, *Kylie*, quickly followed and throughout 1988 the charts were rarely free of her infectious, high-energy pop for long. With 13 consecutive top ten hits, she had the most successful start to a chart career of any woman. When *Kylie* came out, she also became the first solo woman to top the album charts. Despite this, if she'd thought that life as an international pop star would be easier than life as a soap star, she was wrong.

"I've never seen such a punishing schedule," said Pete Waterman in an interview with *Vogue*. "She'd fly in from Australia, looking half asleep, then grab your attention by doing five great tracks in 24 hours, and fly straight back. And she always seemed so frail – like she'd break if you picked her up and hugged her – but she had this incredible stamina."

Of course, some of the flack that S/A/W picked up for their production-line writing techniques was deflected on to Kylie. One Saturday morning kids' TV show even did an experiment where they played a record by S/A/W star Rick Astley at a faster speed. It sounded an awful lot like Kylie, but Pete Waterman didn't care what people thought. "When people ask me if Kylie Minogue is really Rick Astley speeded up," he smirked to *Smash Hits*. "I tell them that it's really Margaret

"KYLIE"

I've never thought of myself as a great singer.
I'm an okay singer. I can do a lot of things okay.
Which is why I still have a career.

Thatcher and because of who she is she can't put her name on the record!"

In fact, all Stock, Aitken and Waterman records sounded fairly similar. Pete Waterman had modelled his production company on the great soul writers of Motown, delighting in the fact that he had a recognisable house style, even if it wasn't a style that won much critical acclaim. However, although Kylie always respected what S/A/W did for her, she couldn't help but feel frustrated by her lack of creative input. "I was a puppet in the beginning. I don't argue with that," she admitted in 1990 when she first began to break free. "That was my education and my payment to get into this world."

"For so many years it was all, 'Can she sing?/Can't she sing?'" she said more recently, "and I've never thought of myself as a great singer. I'm an okay singer. I can do a lot of things okay. Which is why I still have a career."

By the time Kylie had enjoyed that record-breaking run of 13 hits in three years, she was a very different woman from the naive girl who'd flown in from Australia. She'd left *Neighbours* following Scott and Charlene's wedding, she'd started going out partying more often in London and, for her 13th hit 'Shocked', she'd unveiled a much more risque image. In the eyes of the media, and as British music magazine *NME* once put it, Kylie was slowly morphing into SexKylie.

Opposite: Kylie sparkles at the Antwerp Diamond Awards. *Below:* Kylie, Jason and Bros try to 'Feed The World' at the second coming of Bob Geldof's charity event, 1989.

SEXKYLIE:

FROM JASON DONOVAN TO MICHAEL HUTCHENCE

CHAPTER FOUR 4

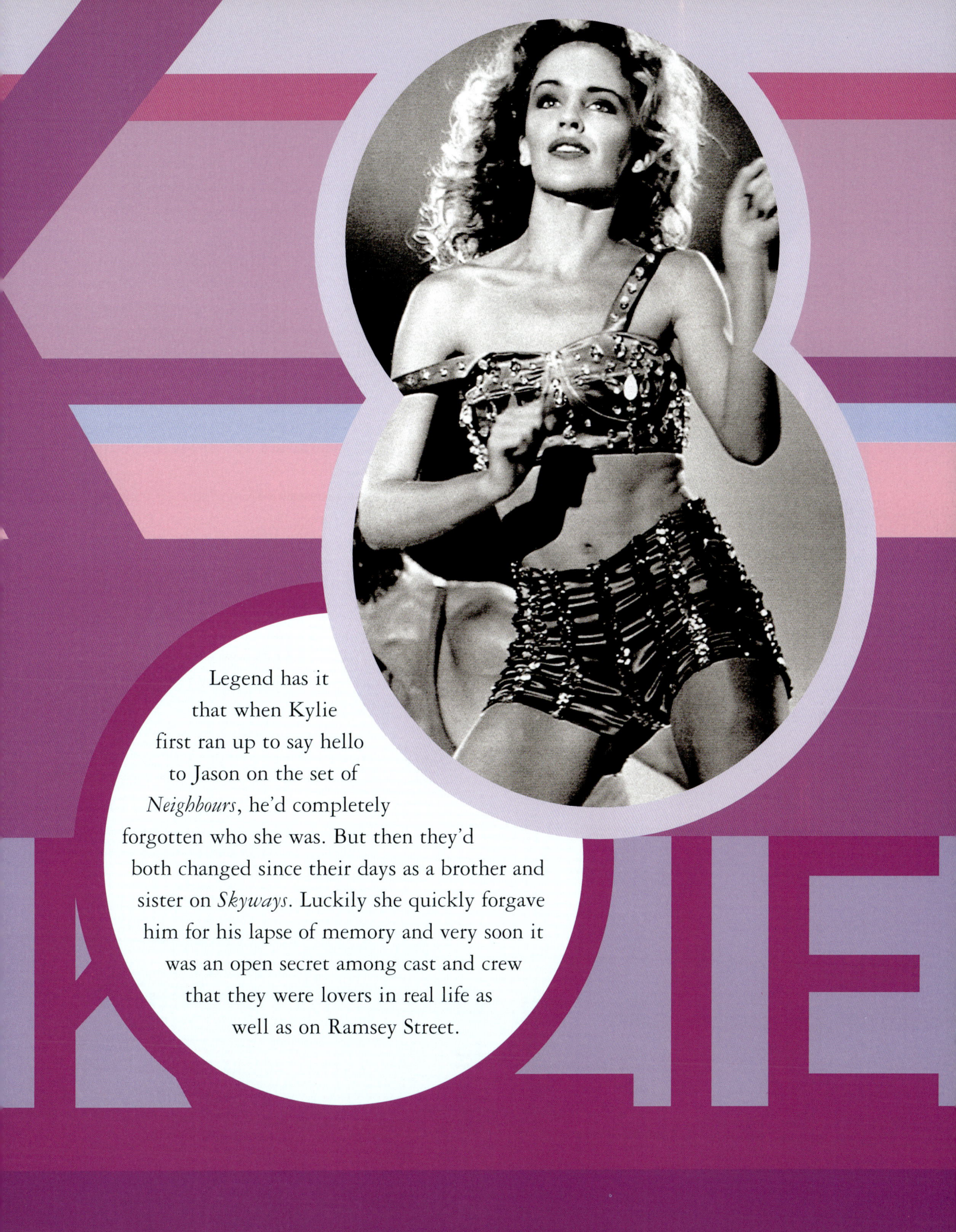

Legend has it that when Kylie first ran up to say hello to Jason on the set of *Neighbours*, he'd completely forgotten who she was. But then they'd both changed since their days as a brother and sister on *Skyways*. Luckily she quickly forgave him for his lapse of memory and very soon it was an open secret among cast and crew that they were lovers in real life as well as on Ramsey Street.

Time to choose:
Jason Donovan ...

Of course, this was confusing for those who have trouble distinguishing soap characters from the actors who play them. Vivian Gray, who played busybody Mrs Mangel in the early years of *Neighbours*, was sometimes booed by dimwit fans when she went out in public. In Kylie and Jason's case a similar affliction seemed to affect much of Fleet Street. Rarely have actors been so closely identified with their characters. The producers had deliberately set out to blur the lines between fantasy and reality with a series of promotional appearances throughout Australia and later the UK.

When *Neighbours'* bosses found out about the relationship between their two stars, they allegedly advised Kylie and Jason to keep it quiet. As a result, intentionally or not, there was a constant stream of speculation in the newspapers. "It was a crazy time for us," said Kylie afterwards to Australian magazine *New Idea*. "We were so young and we were thrust into this mad world when we still had so much growing up to do. I have mainly fond memories of that time. But we worked so hard then, harder than I'll probably ever work now, and Jason was a big part of my life at that time. When we were seeing each other, it was the ever-present question: 'Are you together?' And we didn't try to admit or deny it. We wanted to keep our relationship to ourselves."

Fans wanted Kylie and Jason to be just like Scott and Charlene and yet for a long time neither party would confirm the truth. It wasn't until style magazine *The Face* printed a poster alleging that Jason Donovan was gay that the real story came out. In one of the most counter-productive libel actions of recent times, he sued and, despite the fact that he won a huge settlement, he ended up being considered a figure of fun at best and a homophobe at worst. In an ill-judged attempt to redress the balance, he then spilt the beans in an interview with Radio One disc jockey Steve Wright. Not only was he not gay, he informed a startled nation, but he'd also been Kylie Minogue's boyfriend for almost four years.

Apparently Kylie wasn't amused. In the past she'd always been keen to let everyone know the truth but Jason had tried to wrap things up. She has said that Jason was never quite as bland as his public persona suggested. "He's quite eccentric," she told *FHM*, "and I don't know how much people are aware of that. All people seem to read are reports that he's not the same old Jason he was ten years ago and that he keeps collapsing. Well, yes, he has collapsed a few times, but it's not like he hasn't got anything left in his life. He's a bit mad, however. And I have to say he's very, very funny. People think he takes himself seriously and I'm sure in some ways he does, but there's another side to him that's quite loony and out there."

The couple sometimes found the tensions between life on screen and off difficult to deal with. When the relationship was finally over, Kylie said, "For too long my relationships were mixed in with work and I really didn't know where the line was." There was a deep bond between Kylie and Jason because they had been through such similar experiences and yet, as she grew up, he soon became an unfortunate reminder of a time in her life she was anxious to forget. Think of Kylie and Jason and you think of a wholesome relationship, some highly unfortunate outfits and a public image that was much more twee and saccharine than the reality.

For Kylie, the first great love of her life came along just in time. In 1989 Michael Hutchence was at the peak of his powers. His band, INXS, had just released their best and most successful album *Kick* and he was widely regarded as the closest thing the late 1980s had to an out-and-out rock star. INXS was certainly the first Australian rock band to make it big since

... or Michael Hutchence?

AC/DC years before and they were revered in their home country.

To begin with, though, it seems that Michael regarded the supposedly innocent pop puppet as little more than an interesting challenge. In his world, her brand of Stock, Aitken and Waterman-composed pop was anathema. Until he met her he'd believed that she was merely the gawky ingenue of the tabloids' imagination, but that impression would very quickly change.

At the end of 1989 Kylie was about to begin her debut world tour. The first date would be in Osaka, Japan, but she was spending a few days in Hong Kong on the way. Michael heard about this and through a mutual friend he offered to show her around. He'd lived in the city for the first few years of his life and he often went back there.

The date didn't start well for the shaggy-haired rock star. He was very late arriving at her hotel room to meet her and he was confronted by the glares of Kylie's mother, four dancers, her assistant and her manager. "They were getting more and more protective and annoyed," laughed Kylie later in an interview with the *Telegraph*. "He finally arrived and was confronted by all these angry faces."

In fact, far from being as casual as he'd appeared, Michael Hutchence had travelled all the way from Australia to see her and, as Kylie

"KYLIE

I was 21 when I started dating Michael and I've always said that it was like I had blinkers on and he took them off. "

reported in Vincent Lovegrove's 1999 biography of the INXS star, his plan eventually worked. "We went out and must have stayed out talking in the streets of Hong Kong till four or five in the morning," she told the author. "We just hit it off amazingly well. But I wouldn't let him kiss me, which probably drove him crazy."

The besotted star then started sending her flowers and calling her all the time and very soon they were together – at least as often as their crowded schedules would allow. They had a few snatched days in Tokyo in October and in November 1989 they managed to spend a week in a hotel room at the end of the tour. As you can imagine, Jason was devastated. Much later he said, in a rather ungentlemanly turn of phrase, that he was "gutted … because I was in there first".

"I guess it's up to every individual as to how much you want to remain private," responded a dignified Kylie, "and he has been private for many years. I'm not disappointed, that's life. Maybe one day I'll talk about things I never ever thought I would," she continued in an interview with *New Idea* magazine. "There's a reason for everything. I'm not mad at him for talking about it. Obviously he has his reasons and we still see each other every now and then, but we don't know about one another's lives."

Opposite: Michael liked to while away the hours playing noughts and crosses.
Right: Not such a tomboy any more, 1989.

These days Kylie describes her meeting with Michael Hutchence as one of the key events of her life. "I was 21 when I started dating Michael and I've always said that it was like I had blinkers on and he took them off," she told *Metro*. For the first few months that they were together, their relationship proceeded at a chaotic, whirlwind pace. Kylie would persuade her long-suffering manager Terry Blamey to arrange promotional duties in Frankfurt one weekend and Hong Kong the next, anything to make her schedule coincide with Michael's. "It was shocking for everyone, including me," admitted Kylie later, "but he wasn't as bad as everyone thought, and I wasn't as good. We met somewhere in the middle."

Left: Kylie always said she'd make a good secretary.
Opposite: Celebrating Michael's birthday in 1990.

49

Above: Kylie tantalises Paris, 1990.
Opposite: John Lennon tribute concert, Liverpool, 1990.

" It was shocking for everyone, including me, but Michael wasn't as bad as everyone thought, and I wasn't as good. We met somewhere in the middle. "

KYLIE

Taking control in
Birmingham, 1990.

This new-found sense of liberation was both exaggerated and simplified by the press into a new cliché: Kylie, the innocent pop poppet, being corrupted and moulded by the big bad rock star. Admittedly, some of the couple's comments did little to squash this myth. "I don't know what we should do first," he supposedly said when they first met, "have lunch or have sex." On another occasion he listed "corrupting Kylie" as one of his hobbies. Further evidence was provided by customs officials who supposedly discovered a pair of handcuffs in her luggage.

Stock, Aitken and Waterman certainly knew what they thought. They've since admitted that one of their most popular and acclaimed songs, 'Better The Devil You Know', was written directly about her decision to ditch Jason Donovan for Michael Hutchence. Whether Kylie knew this when she recorded it is not known.

However, there was much more to their relationship than just sex. When she was going out with Michael in 1990, she told Australian magazine *Follow Me*, "Michael just sort of encourages me to be myself, to go after my dreams, to go for what I want. I think that is the most important thing … he gives me confidence. He knows a lot anyway, so he can give me advice."

Unfortunately their relationship didn't last. Both of them were touring regularly and, when they were at home, they were under pressure to come up with the constant stream of new "product" that the record industry demanded. Plus there were always rumours that he was seeing other girls and she finally discovered that he'd been dating supermodel Helena Christensen for many months.

However, even then she still wanted to make the relationship work somehow. When it finally ended she said, "It was one of those situations where you're not sure why you broke up but

you did." The two stars went their separate ways but eventually they did have a reconciliation of sorts. By then she had a new boyfriend and he was with TV presenter Paula Yates, but at least they could be friends.

Then, tragically, in 1997 Michael Hutchence was found dead in a hotel room in Australia. Kylie and everybody else who knew him was devastated, particularly when the coroner recorded a verdict of suicide. Since then there have been claims that he asphyxiated himself in a bizarre sex game, but nobody knows what really happened.

On the morning of the funeral, she was one of a number of glamorous exes who gathered at St Andrew's Cathedral in Sydney to say goodbye. She had always wondered what would have happened if they'd stayed together and now she would never know. That morning, she says, she did feel as though he was watching over her. "I've never gone into it in detail because it's too personal," she told *The Face*. "But I had a real amazing experience: just a feeling and a reaction in my body, and what I felt he was saying was, 'It's OK.' It was comforting."

Trying to control her feelings at Michael Hutchence's funeral in 1997.

SPREADING HER **WINGS**

SPREADING HER WINGS

CHAPTER **5** FIVE

KYLIE

SPREADING HER WINGS

Although their
relationship didn't
last, Michael Hutchence
had a huge influence on
Kylie's life. After she met him,
her first attempt to break out from
the shadow of Charlene Mitchell came
when she starred in the aptly named film
The Delinquents. She played a feisty country
girl called Lola Lovell growing up in
the rapidly changing Australia
of the late 1950s.

Whereas Charlene Mitchell's rebelliousness in *Neighbours* consisted of talking back to adults and wearing overalls, Lola Lovell's feistiness took the form of smoking (shock) and having sex (horror). Inevitably, the British press had a field day with the idea of the super-sweet, innocent Kylie portraying such an "outrageous" character.

It was the first time she'd ever had the opportunity to act outside the constraints of cheap, daytime television. For once she was able to think about the character and take her time to get every scene right. It was a revelation for her. "That was a catalyst," she told *Gay Times*. "I turned 21 in the middle of filming and I was quite proud of what I'd done. It gave me a lot of inspiration and confidence to think that maybe I could do more. Before the release of the film, I started going out with Michael and I was slowly becoming a woman. When I started going out with him I didn't even wear lipstick."

Despite some carping from critics about the use of a "soap actress", the film became a big success and Kylie looked forward to many more such roles. However, although she received dozens of scripts, none of them was worth interrupting her career in music for. Recently she was asked if she regretted not doing more

"

KYLIE

Before the release of *The Delinquents*, I started going out with Michael and I was slowly becoming a woman. When I started going out with him I didn't even wear lipstick.

"

films. "Well," she replied, "I have some regrets, but the roles I was getting – I mean, who wouldn't give them up?"

Kylie has always been a perfectionist and at that time she wasn't prepared to do something substandard just for the sake of appearing on the big screen. She took acting very seriously and, after the cheap and cheerful world of *Neighbours*, if she was going to do it she wanted to do it well. "I have a lot of insecurities about my performances," she said many years later to *New Idea*. "But I guess that's why I keep going. I always want to be better. I wouldn't say I'm confident when it comes to acting in movies, and I make it even more difficult because I'm very hard on myself."

The process of making *The Delinquents* had stirred her creative juices and she returned to music determined to have a greater creative input. To begin with, Stock, Aitken and Waterman were understandably sceptical about this. After all, even Mike Stock and Matt Aitken had been through many years of learning their trade before they became the most prolific hit-makers of the 1980s. They must have inwardly groaned every time one of their stars thought that they could just pick up the same skills overnight.

When it came time to record her second album *Enjoy Yourself* in 1989, the hitmen were still very much in control and, inevitably, Kylie had another huge hit. This must have made the decision to start writing songs herself very difficult. By now, though, Pete Waterman recognised that Kylie was unlike all the other starlets in his stable. "On her first LP, she'd basically walked straight out of a soap opera and into a recording studio," he explained to *Vox* magazine in 1990. "But she's getting older and obviously more worldly wise and, since she doesn't live in Australia that much, she's going out and absorbing a much wider range of influences."

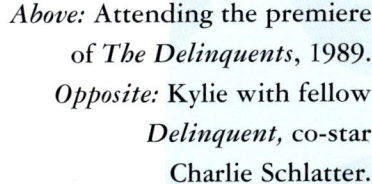

Above: Attending the premiere of *The Delinquents,* 1989.
Opposite: Kylie with fellow *Delinquent,* co-star Charlie Schlatter.

Above and opposite:
**Kylie shocks
Plymouth, 1991.**

Before writing songs for herself, Kylie wrote a song for somebody else to sing. It was called 'Love Traffic' and it appeared on her sister Dannii's debut album. This move did two things. Firstly, it squashed rumours of a rivalry between the two siblings, and secondly it demonstrated to S/A/W and the world that she could write if she wanted to.

For the first time, like *Neighbours* before him, Pete Waterman was having to accept that one of his stars might be bigger than the stable that had spawned her. "I honestly don't think there's anything this girl can't do if she sets her heart on it," he said presciently, "and in that respect, she's probably the same as Madonna. She was never just a soap star. This girl has grown in stature all the way down the line, and she's taken her audience with her."

The biggest leap for her audience came with the release of her raunchiest single and video yet, 'Shocked'. At the age of 23, Kylie wasn't just breaking down people's preconceptions about her, she was shattering them into pieces. The woolly jumper-wearing girl-next-door had suddenly turned into a whip-wielding, leather-clad dominatrix.

"There are some shocking scenes in it," Pete Waterman admitted (or boasted) at the time in the same *Vox* interview. "I'm an old man now and I'm not quite sure my heart can take it. If it has that effect on me, and I've known her for five years and see her at least twice a week, it's got to have the same effect on someone who only sees her on video or television."

Unfortunately the video backfired in one sense. Her American record company MCA decided that the video for 'Shocked' was rather too shocking for American consumers and they refused to release the single in the States. Ironically, her career wouldn't recover across the Atlantic until she came out with the even more seductive 'Can't Get You Out Of My Head'.

Despite this, however, Kylie was enjoying the most artistically satisfying period of her musical career so far. She might not have been in complete control but, compared with what she was used to, the new-found freedom was heaven. On her third album, *Rhythm Of Love*, she worked with a whole range of songwriters, including people who'd written for the likes of Madonna and Paula Abdul. They, it's fair to say, didn't keep their stars sitting in the lobby while they scribbled songs to order. "People I've been writing with might ask, 'Oh, what do you think?'" Kylie gushed to *Follow Me* magazine. "And I'll say, 'Who me? What do I think? Oh, wow!' At Stock, Aitken and Waterman they'd write the song and I'd sing it and it was that simple."

This might sound like she was criticising the hit-makers but Kylie has always acknowledged the debt she owes to S/A/W. It's just that as she got older she understandably wanted more control over her career and, although they were still phenomenally successful by anybody else's standards, S/A/W weren't quite the force in the 1990s that they had been in the previous decade. Matt Aitken left the company in 1991 and, for her fourth and final studio album for PWL, Kylie insisted on co-writing with Mike Stock.

> "I honestly don't think there's anything this girl can't do if she sets her heart on it ... She was never just a soap star. This girl has grown in stature all the way down the line, and she's taken her audience with her."

Opposite: Are you having fun yet? *Left:* ...You'd better be!

61

The result, *Let's Get To It*, immediately suffered one of the worst fates that any album can experience if it wants to be a big commercial success: it was a huge critical success. Writers in the broadsheets and the serious music press, who'd generally disdained, patronised or ignored Kylie's earlier work, loved it. Inevitably, *Let's Get To It* was the first of her records not to go top ten.

Opposite and below: Who's that girl – Kylie or Madonna?

Soon after, Kylie faced a new and unexpected attack. She'd always admitted that Madonna was an enormous inspiration to her but now some critics were saying that she'd overstepped the mark towards outright imitation. This was largely because of her Madonna-style preference for underwear as outerwear on the *Let's Get To It* tour. Of course, as Kylie has often demurely said, too many clothes just look silly on someone as petite as her.

For a time it seemed that her sister Dannii was a serious rival for the princess of pop crown. Dannii was at the same point in her career that Kylie had been three years before. She had no baggage or preconceptions to deal with and she was just happy to sing the songs she was given and try to have hits. Inevitably the rumours of rivalry, that had dogged the two sisters ever since Kylie won the role of Carla in *The Sullivans,* resurfaced.

They wouldn't be human if they didn't experience the odd twang of jealousy but both sisters have always denied that there's any animosity between them. "We just laugh at all that," said Kylie. The two sisters even did an interview for men's lifestyle magazine *Esquire,* saucily playing on the frisson created by the two famous sex symbols together.

"Whenever people ask me what my sister is like," Dannii explained, "I think of us as cartoon characters. Kylie is a fluffy, purring pussycat, and I'm like a bulldog. Both have their strengths. Sometimes I have wished I didn't bulldoze quite as much in every situation. I wish I could be a little more flirty and free. A bit more pussycat."

By now, though, there was a serious risk that Kylie's career was drawing to a close. She'd already had far more success than anyone would have predicted after 'I Should Be So Lucky'. She had one more album to release for PWL, a greatest hits collection, and that was that. The future was far from clear. Various record companies were interested in signing her, but she was bored with being the malleable naif of old. It was time for a change of direction.

Something from Oz at the World Music Awards, 1991.

What well-dressed eco-warriors wore at the 1995 Rainforest Fashion Show, London.

"KYLIE"

Whenever people ask me what my sister is like,
I think of us as cartoon characters. Kylie is a fluffy,
purring pussycat, and I'm like a bulldog.

DANCE KYLIE or INDIE KYLIE?

CHAPTER 6 SIX

Even by the end of 1989, her second year with PWL, Kylie had already made an estimated £5 million gross from record sales. When it came time to look for a new deal in 1992, it's safe to assume that she didn't have too many money worries. She could afford to put creative freedom at the top of her shopping list. The first label to offer her this was ultra-hip dance imprint deConstruction.

Above: Get me out of here: Kylie with Jean-Claude Van Damme in *Streetfighter.* *Opposite:* Just one more picture then. At the 1994 World Music Awards.

From the explosion of acid house in the late 1980s, dance music had been taking over from pure pop as the dominant force in the charts and deConstruction were at the forefront. They lured her with the promise that she would work with some of the finest talent around and she would be re-made as a "dance diva".

They were as good as their word – maybe too good. Kylie's previous albums had been dashed off in the DIY spirit of Stock, Aitken and Waterman – fast, fun and frothy – but deConstruction wanted to show that they were taking her seriously. They gathered together some of the most successful names in dance pop, including Brothers in Rhythm, Rapino Brothers, M People, St Etienne and the Pet Shop Boys, and they set them loose to fight among themselves. "I felt like a ping pong

ball for a while," said Kylie ruefully, "with American and English producers both wanting different things."

After some pruning, the album that emerged, *Kylie Minogue,* was a successful blend of dance beats, modern R&B and pop sensibilities. The first single 'Confide In Me' is still a favourite of many fans and, although it didn't sell in the vast numbers of her work with PWL, it did gain the grudging respect of critics. The original plan to re-create Kylie as a sophisticated artist was a qualified success.

Of course, looking back from 2002 we might wonder why Kylie ever wanted to be seen as anything other than the great pop star that she is, but for most of the 1990s she was still very uncomfortable with memories of her early career. Flitting from one project to another,

KYLIE

I felt like a ping pong ball for a while, with American and English producers both wanting different things.

Conquering the clubbers at Liverpool nightclub Cream's second birthday.

she couldn't seem to decide what she wanted to be. One moment she was trying to crack Hollywood in the dreadful Jean-Claude Van Damme vehicle *Streetfighter*, the next she was playing a psychotic drug addict in the short art film *Hayride To Hell*.

In one of the biggest twists of her career, it would be critically acclaimed Australian singer-songwriter Nick Cave who would give Kylie the confidence to accept her past. The two singers had grown up minutes from each other in Melbourne but their early lives could hardly have been more different. As Kylie once put it, "When I was merrily singing 'I Should Be So Lucky', Nick was just going into rehab."

Although he'd started his career in the early 1980s with the extraordinarily violent and chaotic punk group The Birthday Party, Nick

had mellowed in recent years and he'd developed a fascination with the sadness at the heart of so many great love songs. As he pointed out, 'I Should Be So Lucky', like so many seemingly chirpy pop songs, is lyrically very downbeat and sad. The point is that the innocent singer doesn't get the object of her affections and she doesn't think she ever will.

Nick had been writing songs for Kylie for years, but it wasn't until 1995 that he plucked up the courage to present her with one of them. They were both at home in Australia staying with their respective parents and for a time their mothers acted as answer machines while they tried to hook up. He was in the middle of recording his most morbid album yet, the self-explanatory *Murder Ballads*. She was just enjoying a holiday. As a friend of Michael

Hutchence, Nick knew that there was more to Kylie than met the eye and he wanted her to sing the part of doomed lover Eliza Day in a new song 'Where The Wild Roses Grow'.

Eventually the two singers got together and, perhaps to their surprise, they found that they had much more in common than they'd thought. Kylie said later to *Metro*, "I'd somehow developed this relationship with Nick whereby he would sometimes call me up and say, 'Hey, I'm doing something tomorrow and I've just written this song and I'd like you to sing the chorus for me. Okay? I'll see you tomorrow!'"

'Where The Wild Roses Grow' was very different from anything she'd done before, but it was tuneful enough to appeal to her old fans and dark enough to impress Nick Cave's gothic followers. It didn't do as well as anything from her PWL years but nobody expected it to. A chart position of number 11 was considered highly respectable. Meanwhile, she and Nick had become good friends and they stayed in contact.

In 1996 at the Royal Albert Hall in London, Nick gave Kylie the chance to exorcise some of her demons. It was at an event called the Poetry Olympics. Nick was to be there reading some of his own lyrics and he suggested she come down and recite one of the songs she'd made famous – 'I Should Be So Lucky' perhaps? She told him she'd think about it but inwardly she was mortified. How would the cream of London's literati react to Kylie Minogue turning up at their highbrow poetry shindig?

However, Nick was more persuasive than she thought and at last she found herself backstage, almost shaking with fear, as acclaimed artists like Patti Smith recited their work to the literary throng. At last it was almost her turn. There was just one speaker before her, a bearded, blind man who was reading his work from braille. In a panic

With fellow sex symbol Elton John at the Stonewall Equality Show.

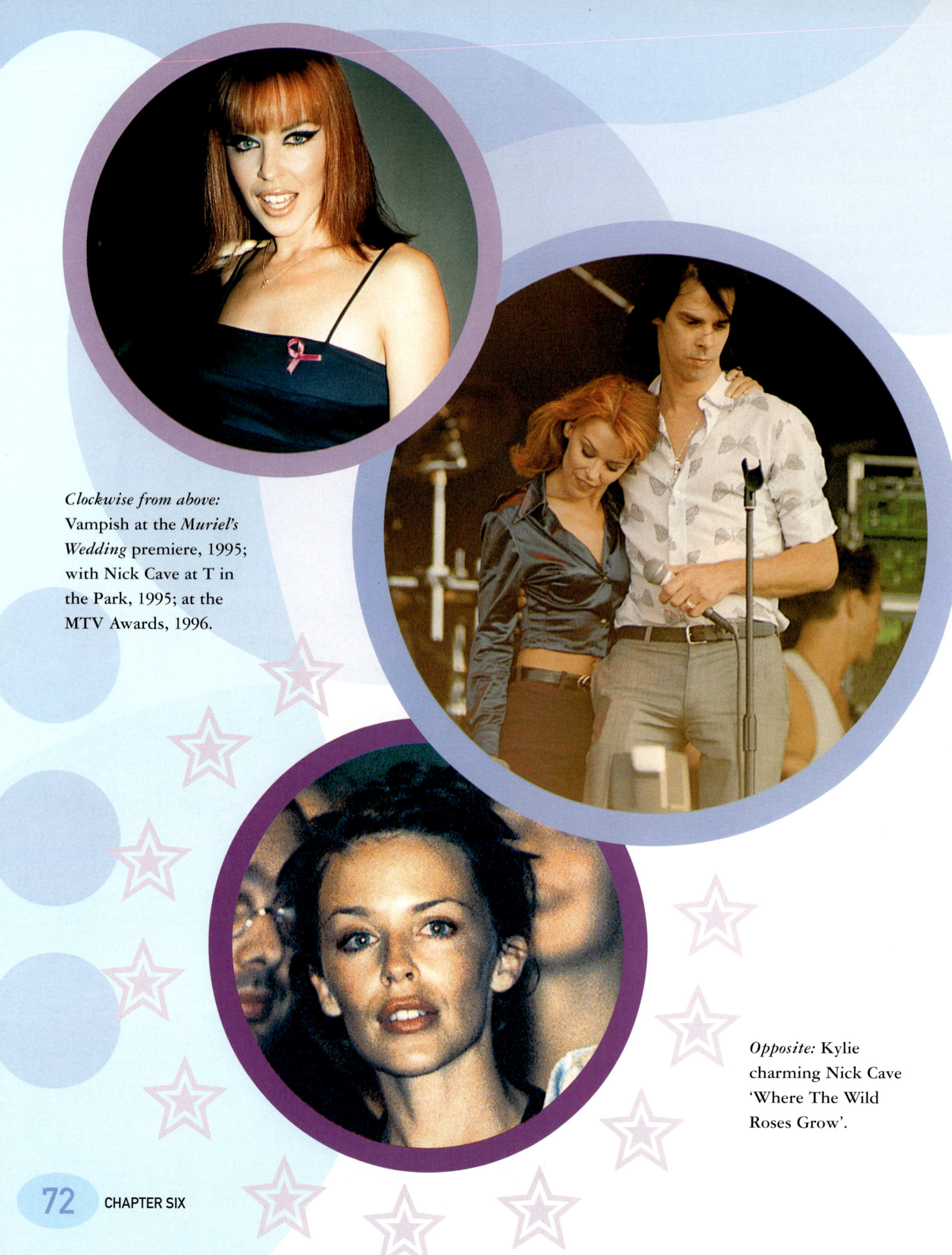

Clockwise from above:
Vampish at the *Muriel's Wedding* premiere, 1995; with Nick Cave at T in the Park, 1995; at the MTV Awards, 1996.

Opposite: Kylie charming Nick Cave 'Where The Wild Roses Grow'.

Above: Pretending to be dead for Nick Cave, Brixton, 1996. *Opposite:* **Pretending to be indie for The Manic Street Preachers, Shepherd's Bush Empire, 1996.**

she turned to Nick Cave and said, "Nick, God is on stage! How am I supposed to follow that?" Follow it she did, though. With the applause for the blind man just fading away around the auditorium, she strode bravely out on to stage and began to speak: "In my imagination / There is no complication / I dream about you all the time …"

"The reaction of the audience was amazing," Kylie told *Metro*. "It was such an important moment and it was completely different from anything I'd ever done. I was in my tracksuit pants without a scrap of make-up on, with a sticker with my name written on it. It was a really cathartic moment for me. I felt like I was face-to-face with the young girl who was once me."

Kylie was flattered by the new-found respect she was receiving. At that time the boundaries between what was considered pop and what was considered alternative were narrowing. Bands like Oasis, Blur and Pulp were topping the British charts and pop music with guitars seemed to be approaching the status of dance as a commercial force. Meanwhile Kylie had become an icon who could offer her collaborators what she'd never been able to offer before: a kind of post-modern cool.

It was a commodity that was very much in demand. In December 1996, successful Welsh indie band the Manic Street Preachers were playing a gig at London's Shepherd's Bush Empire. Already their fans were divided into two factions: the "old manics" fans who held true to the band's heavy, punk roots and the "new manics" fans who loved that year's more poppy tunes. The old fans were about to get a shock. Halfway through the gig Kylie Minogue stepped on to the stage and began singing a song called 'Little Baby Nothing'. The Manics had written it for her back in 1992 but then, of course, they were relatively unknown and she was experimenting with dance music and it didn't happen. By 1996 the whole musical landscape had shifted.

If it was a shock for the indie crowd, Kylie fans didn't know what to think either. Had they lost her to the alternative crowd forever? How long would it be before she started wearing Doc Marten boots and drinking cider?

More shocks were to follow. In 1997 Kylie went into the studio with James Dean Bradfield of the Manics to record a new album. Just like her first effort for deConstruction, the sessions were chaotic, with collaborators swinging in through one door and out the other. Everybody thought that they knew what Kylie should do next and for a time she couldn't decide which path to follow. As a result, *Impossible Princess*, as it was to be called, was wildly eclectic, swinging from the indie of Bradfield's 'A Kind Of Bliss' to more dancey tracks. It's most notable now for some of the most personal and downbeat lyrics Kylie has ever written.

" The reaction of the audience was amazing …
It was a really cathartic moment for me. I felt like
I was face-to-face with the young girl who was once me. "

"It wasn't a happy time in my life. I felt I was alone ... Definitely on some songs, lyrically it's obvious to me now that I am saying, 'I'm not waving. I am, in fact, drowning. Hello? Is anybody there?'"

"That album was difficult," she said to *Rolling Stone* magazine. "It wasn't a happy time in my life. I felt I was alone. I didn't have the help I needed. Definitely on some songs, lyrically it's obvious to me now that I am saying, 'I'm not waving. I am, in fact, drowning. Hello? Is anybody there?' At the time I felt like there was no one to help me. I didn't have the support of the record company. Nothing gelled on that record."

In fact the album had its fans, not least Madonna who reportedly considered signing Kylie to her record label in America, but commercially it was by far her biggest flop in the UK. In the first two weeks it only sold 20,000 copies, far less than any of her previous works. It wasn't helped by the fact that, shortly before the release date, Princess Diana died in a car crash, making the name seem much more topical than it was ever meant to be. In Australia it was too late to change it and the album did very well but in Britain it was bizarrely changed to *Kylie Minogue* – despite the fact that her last album had also been called *Kylie Minogue*.

As always Kylie is her own harshest critic but she now accepts that even IndieKylie had some things going for her. "It might be an album that in a few years some people will listen to a bit more," she said recently. "I think there's definitely some good parts on the album, I just don't think it was cohesive at all. At least it's an indication of that time in my life. It isn't pretending anything." It was just one of the many different versions of Kylie.

Left: Casual glamour at the Elle Style Awards.
Opposite: Reading to London's literati at the ICA, 1997.

THE MANY DIFFERENT

KYLIE

KYLIE

DIFFERENT

KYLIES

SEVEN

CHAPTER

7

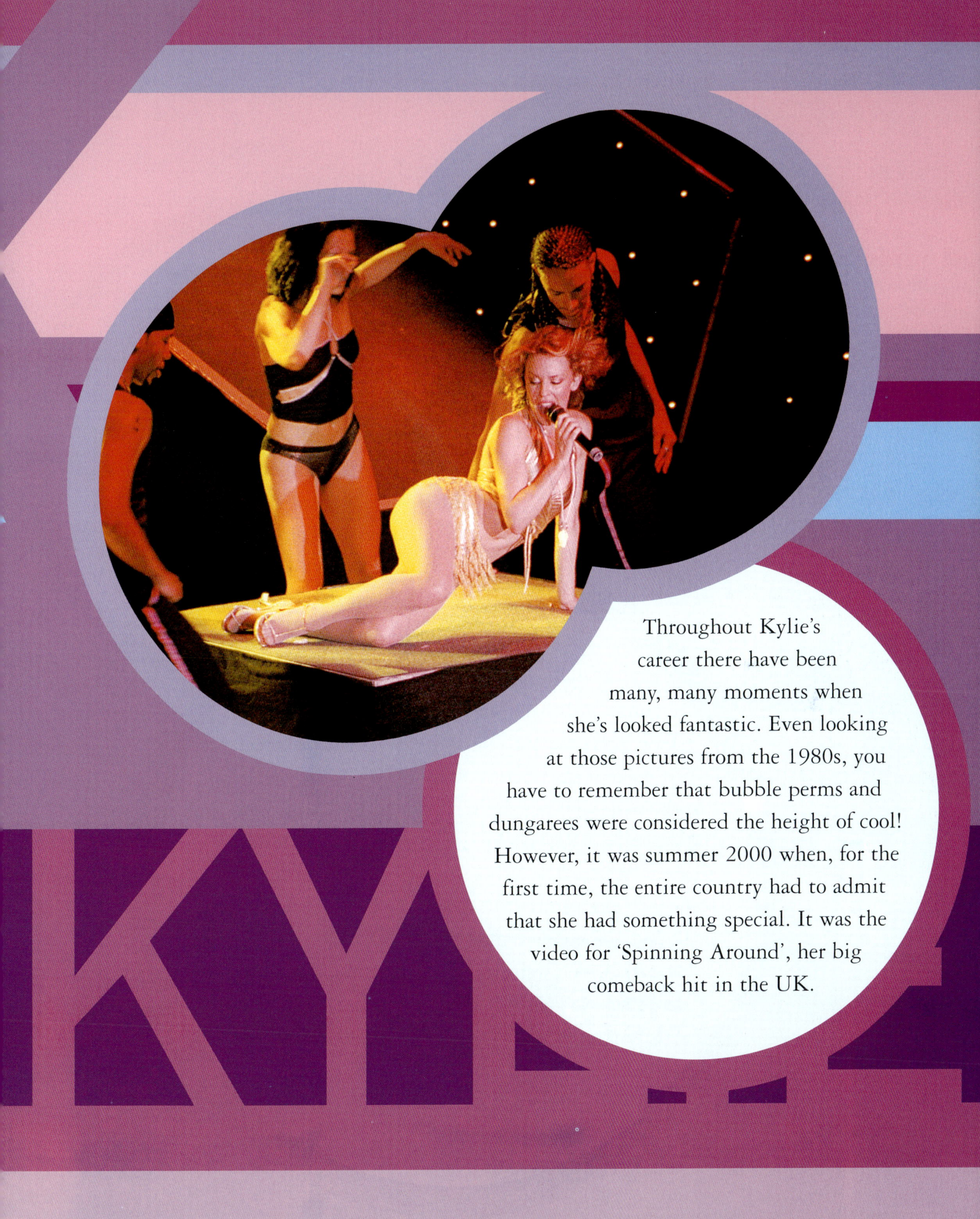

Throughout Kylie's career there have been many, many moments when she's looked fantastic. Even looking at those pictures from the 1980s, you have to remember that bubble perms and dungarees were considered the height of cool! However, it was summer 2000 when, for the first time, the entire country had to admit that she had something special. It was the video for 'Spinning Around', her big comeback hit in the UK.

In the video Kylie's dancing on the bar, wearing the smallest, shiniest pair of hot pants ever seen on national television and, right there, a sartorial legend is born. "I think my gold hot pants stole the show," Kylie says. "I don't think I get noticed at all. Those little hot pants have a life of their own and they're off and running."

Not true, of course. The hot pants, supposedly bought for 50p in an Oxfam shop, were only half the story. It wasn't even the fact that she has a preternaturally perfect bottom. Well, OK, that was important, but it was also the fact that for the first time she looked like she was in complete control of the way she looked, the way she dressed and the way she acted.

"I am proud of that video," she says. "All that stuff on the bar was just someone saying to me, 'Y'know what? Just make it up.' And something just came over me!" In the past, whether she was covered in bubble bath for the 'I Should Be So Lucky' video or playing dead for Nick Cave in 'Where The Wild Roses Grow', there was always somebody else calling the shots. Maybe because Kylie's so small and vulnerable-looking, there's something about her that makes men want to take care of her, to mould her and shape her and get her to "improve" her image. "I think everyone's got a different version, either that they want me to be, or they imagine me to be," she says.

'Spinning Around' and the *Light Years* album proved that she was at her best when working with great talents but also when she was allowed to make the final decision. Over the last 15 years she's been able to get close enough to her fans to know when something works and when it doesn't. "I think there is a very human element to the relationship that my audience and myself have in that I can't double cross them," she told *Arena*. "I don't get away with things when it's not really me, or when I make mistakes they kind of go, 'Oh, she's going through a phase, she'll come to her senses.'"

However, she hasn't given up listening to good advice. For the last nine years the most significant influence on her fashion sense has been her friend and official Creative Director Will Baker. Will, the son of a teacher from Cheshire, met Kylie when she came into the Vivienne Westwood shop where he was working. He'd heard that she didn't have a stylist so he'd written to her offering his services, with no real expectation that she'd accept. When she walked into the shop, he immediately seized his chance. He told the *Mirror*: "I just leapt over the counter and bombarded her with ideas. She probably thought I was some mad stalker, but she listened and took me for a coffee over the road."

According to Kylie, "Everyone who meets him finds him unforgettable. Over the years, we have become somewhat joined at the hip and developed a relationship where we collaborate on nearly every creative aspect of my career." Will is the man who found the famous pair of gold hot pants and for that half the country would probably like to buy him a drink.

Her recent victories in the style wars have been about more than just sex. Her gay audience, always highly supportive, were even more impressed by the high-camp in her recent disco diva videos. "There's a part of me that is, and always will be, camp," she agrees. "Or showy – that's probably a better way to put it. And that's what a lot of gay men adore. I'm a drag queen trapped in a woman's body," she said to *Sky* magazine, "A very short drag queen trapped in a woman's body!"

Unusually for a bona fide sex symbol, women love her just as much as men. "When 'Spinning Around' came out I was so surprised," she told *Arena*, "so many girls and women came up to me and said, 'We love your song, and you look so great and so sexy in that video.' That really touched me. That they weren't saying, "Pff, God, pff, what's she doing strutting around in those shorts making us feel insecure?' They weren't like that at all. I was their mate."

Opposite: Style guru Will Baker offers Kylie at few cheeky fashion tips at the 2002 Dolce & Gabbana show.

I am proud of [the 'Spinning Around'] video. All that stuff on the bar was just someone saying to me, 'Y'know what? Just make it up.' And something just came over me!

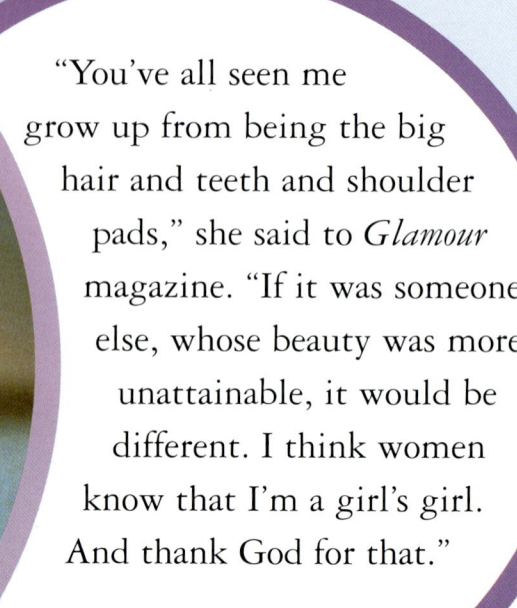

"You've all seen me grow up from being the big hair and teeth and shoulder pads," she said to *Glamour* magazine. "If it was someone else, whose beauty was more unattainable, it would be different. I think women know that I'm a girl's girl. And thank God for that."

Kylie's "attainable" beauty over the years. *Above:* Early 1990s. *Right:* Tower Records, 1997. *Opposite:* Versace party, 1999.

10 GREAT KYLIE IMAGES

1 **SPINNING AROUND video:** *That* video, obviously. The perfect blend of high camp, sophisticated sex and lovable exuberance.

2 **CAN'T GET YOU OUT OF MY HEAD video:** Even if the song hadn't been a work of some genius, the image of Kylie, dress split to the thigh, cheekily toying with the gearstick in her car, would have lived on.

3 **SOME KIND OF BLISS video:** The peak of Indiekylie. Most notable for the denim hot pants that, inadvertently, inspired the 'Spinning Around' look. "One of my producers, Johnny Douglas, said he really liked that video for 'Some Kind Of Bliss'," Kylie says, "and I asked why and he said, 'Well, it was the little denim hot pants.' So I made a mental note."

4 **THE BRIT AWARDS 2002 performance:** £900 silver Jimmy Choo boots, £900 Dolce & Gabbana minidress, £80 Agent Provocateur knickers, £2000 Johnny Rocket jewellery, £400 beauty products and more than £2,000 for her personal hair and make-up people. Kylie's appearance that night came to about £6,000. It was worth it (*see opposite*).

5 **THE OLYMPICS performance:** One billion people saw her performing at the closing ceremony in a fetching feather head-dress. Almost as crucial as 'Can't Get You Out Of My Head' in breaking the US.

6 **WHERE THE WILD ROSES GROW video:** Pale skin, dark hair, white dress and ruby red lips. It's just a shame that in this video Kylie is actually dead. Nick Cave is a great songwriter but a very strange man.

7 **AGENT PROVOCATEUR advert:** "I've really outdone myself this time!" she said, when this highly erotic underwear advert first came out. "I'm basically riding a velvet bronco, wearing black lace knickers, bra, suspenders, stockings, high heels and a slight sweaty glow." It was banned from being shown on TV, unsurprisingly.

8 **I SHOULD BE SO LUCKY video:** OK, she's looked a thousand times better since, but the scenes with Kylie blowing bubbles in the bath demonstrated for the first time her ability to look innocent in the most provocative situations.

9 **THE GREEN FAIRY ABSINTHE in the film MOULIN ROUGE:** Perfectly cast as the sprite who appears when Ewan MacGregor drinks absinthe, Kylie looks amazing. A delighted spokesman for the evil green drink said: "The point about Kylie is that she used to go out with bad boy Michael Hutchence and yet she embodies this innocence, which is what the fairy's about. It's someone who stands between heaven and hell. She's physically perfect as well."

10 **GQ's TENNIS PLAYER SCRATCHING HER BOTTOM magazine cover:** "I saw the contacts of the photos and they were all fine apart from one where I was doing this leaping serve and the skirt I was wearing was sort of fluttering in the breeze and you could see my G-string," she said later. "However, the next time I saw the picture my G-string was no longer there. I was like, 'Who took my knickers off?'"

CHAPTER SEVEN

Above and left: The ultimate showgirl. The closing ceremony of the Sydney Oympics 2000 was watched by a billion people.

SERIAL
MONOGAMY

SERIAL

MONOGAMY

KYLIE

LIE

CHAPTER EIGHT

8

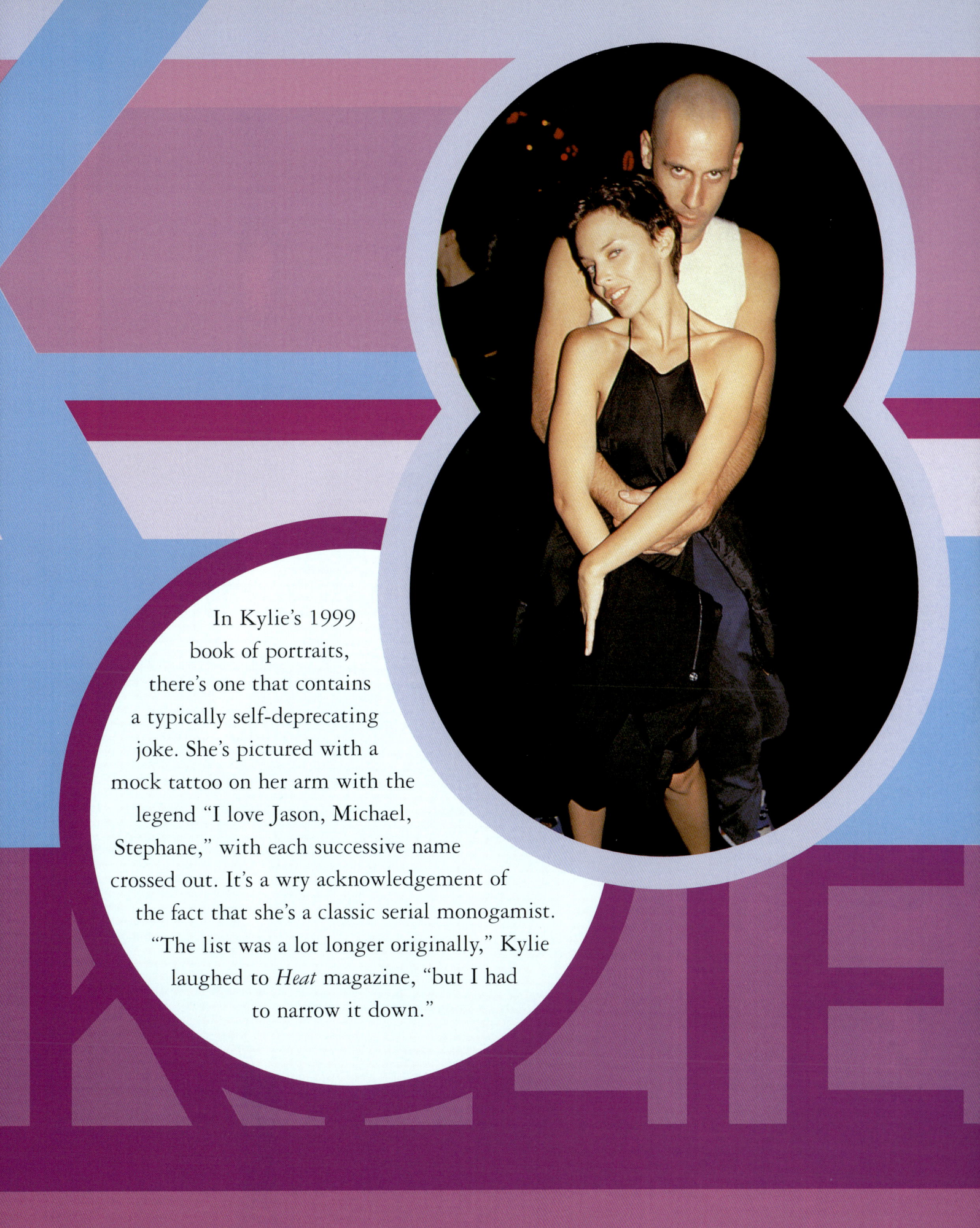

In Kylie's 1999 book of portraits, there's one that contains a typically self-deprecating joke. She's pictured with a mock tattoo on her arm with the legend "I love Jason, Michael, Stephane," with each successive name crossed out. It's a wry acknowledgement of the fact that she's a classic serial monogamist. "The list was a lot longer originally," Kylie laughed to *Heat* magazine, "but I had to narrow it down."

The third man on that list was French photographer Stephane Sednaoui. They met when he took photographs for her first deConstruction album but she fell for him at a packed London party in 1995. It was a hot, sweltering evening and, as the night wore on, the club was getting more and more uncomfortable and claustrophobic. At last her new friend lifted her above his head so that she could breathe and, if she wasn't instantly smitten as some have claimed, she was certainly impressed.

Opposite: A camouflaged Stephane can't understand how the photographers have spotted him.

Not long afterwards it would be Stephane who would accompany her on the fulfilment of one of her childhood ambitions. The two of them hired a Pontiac Trans-Am sportscar and set out to drive across America. It would be one of the happiest experiences of her life.

"KYLIE"

I love Jason, Michael, Stephane … The list was a lot longer originally but I had to narrow it down.

Above: Stephane tries to explain that his dinner jacket's at the dry cleaners. *Opposite:* Ultra-cool at the Q Awards, 2000.

In America almost nobody knew her so the couple were able to travel with an anonymity that was impossible in Europe or Australia. She'd been famous ever since she was 16 years old, but in the States she could live out her own version of the American dream: complete normality. "We were driving from town to town, desert to desert, staying in $20-a-night motels," she told *Cosmopolitan*. "We had greasy breakfasts in roadside cafes and talked to truckers for hours about their lives," she enthused. "It was fun. No one had any preconceived ideas about me. I was truly anonymous and free to be me."

Just as when she'd been going out with Michael she made full use of her wealth, jetting around the world to be with Stephane at a moment's notice. Even so, their's was still a long-distance relationship and, as always, her career meant there was very little time for romance.

He continued to take pictures of her, dazzling her with portraits that made her look like the kind of chic, French actresses she adored. In time, however, the romance wore off and the couple began to drift apart. "I have no problem acknowledging the term 'commitment-phobe'," she's admitted. However, although the tabloids are often full of mock concern about her apparent inability to "keep" a man, it seems more likely that Kylie just doesn't need to "keep" anybody. She's one of the most beautiful, wealthy successful stars in the world. She can afford to be somewhat choosy.

"Most people want to find the right person," she said to *Heat* magazine, "and it eludes you for a long time. There's this minuscule possibility of finding the right person to challenge and inspire you. I meet a lot of amazing men who are adorable, intelligent and funny. But to find someone who has, I don't know what it is, just something …"

10 ALLEGED LIAISONS

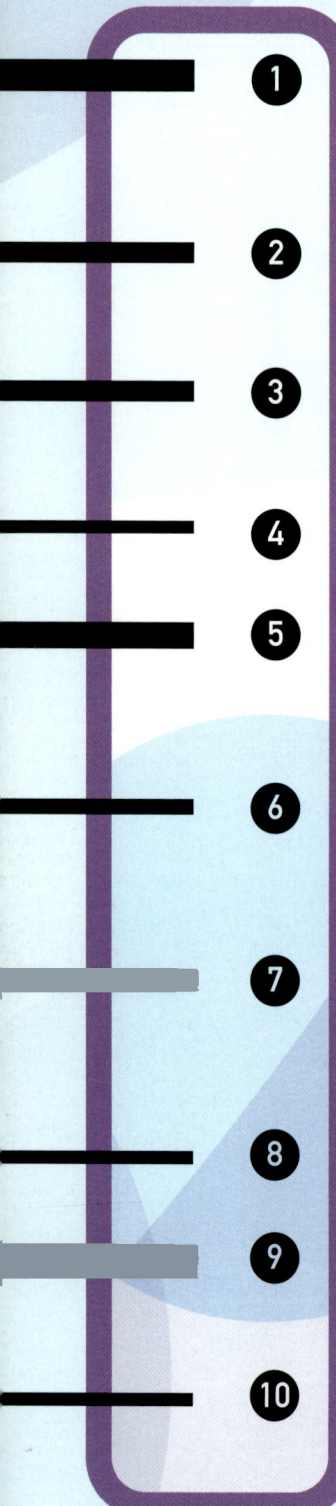

1 **1993 LENNY KRAVITZ:** The Jimi Hendrix-fixated rock star was one of the first men she was linked with after she split up with Michael Hutchence. It's not hard to see that he might have reminded her of Michael, with his love of both rock and leather trousers. Although most rumours about her at that time were untrue, this one apparently has some credibility, even if they never actually went out for long (*see opposite*).

2 **1993–94 ZANE O'DONNELL:** Kylie spent almost a year with the South African model, living in a chic Paris apartment. At the time the papers were full of reports quoting his ex-wife who claimed that he "couldn't resist beautiful women".

3 **1994 EVAN DANDO:** The singer was touring Australia with his band The Lemonheads when he met Kylie. She's never denied that something happened but they were never really going out. "I didn't have anything serious to do with him but there was some frivolity," she's coyly admitted.

4 **1994 JULIAN LENNON:** Apparently he was with his girlfriend when they met at a restaurant in LA but that didn't stop some feverish (and untrue) speculation about the Beatle progeny.

5 **1994 PRINCE:** It's easy to imagine that Prince sits at home scanning the newspapers to find the latest hot young thing to invite back to his place and, if they're somewhere close to his height range like Kylie Minogue, then that must be a bonus, too. However, although the superstar invited her to his Minneapolis mansion Paisley Park, she says that nothing happened.

6 **1995 PAULY SHORE:** Kylie met the American comedy actor on the set of *Bio-Dome*, the film they co-starred in. It seems that, unsurprisingly, he was a lot keener than she was. In the end he was reduced to pleading on his website: "Kylie and I haven't talked for a long time, so if any of you guys in England see her, tell her to f***ing call me. Or at least e-mail me." Unfortunately for him, Stephane Sednaoui had already whisked her off her feet.

7 **1997 JIM CARREY:** Shortly after she split up with Stephane, Jim and Kylie ate in the same restaurant. That this is pretty much the whole story tells you something about the way rumours start for Kylie. "I was at a restaurant in LA and someone at my table knew someone at his table," she told *Heat*. "He asked if I wanted to go over and sit at their table. I did. And that was that."

8 **1998 TIM JEFFRIES:** In the late 1990s it was almost de rigueur for female celebrities to be seen with multi-millionaire and man-about-town Tim Jeffries. Nothing much came of their affair, though.

9 **1999 ROGER LLOYD PACK:** Yes, Kylie was once romantically linked by one newspaper with Trigger from *Only Fools And Horses*. They appeared together in a Barbados production of Shakespeare's *The Tempest* but needless to say there was no truth in the rumour.

10 **1999 RUPERT PENRY JONES:** Kylie met Shakespearean actor Rupert in the same production of *The Tempest*. He played the young hero Ferdinand and she played the squeaky clean heroine Miranda. Pretty soon they were an item but the relationship, another long-distance affair, only lasted a matter of months.

KYLIE

"There's this minuscule possibility of finding the right person ... I meet a lot of amazing men who are adorable, intelligent and funny. But to find someone who has, I don't know what it is, just something ..."

Opposite: Singer Evan Dando goes for the windswept look.
Left: Tim Jeffries thanks God he's a multi-millionaire.
Below: Actor Rupert Penry-Jones does "mean and moody".

RENAISSANCE: KYLIE COMES BACK

KYLIE

CHAPTER NINE

9

After 1997, Kylie could easily have rested on her laurels. She didn't need to keep pushing herself onwards and the last few years had been incredibly draining. She'd earned enough money never to have to work again, apart from the occasional chat show appearance. However, although her career had been more successful than anyone could have imagined, she still wasn't quite satisfied.

There had been so many different Kylies but which one was real? Her early pop incarnation was by far the most successful but, for a long time, she had repudiated that part of her career and that part of her personality. At the beginning of the millennium, though, there were rumours that, she was now ready to make a pure pop album once again.

Inevitably, ears pricked up within the music industry. Pete Waterman was the first to step forward and say that he'd be delighted to work with her again if that was what she wanted. But he misunderstood. Kylie wasn't looking to go back to the old way of doing things. She wanted to have all the best things about her S/A/W years – the frothiness, the fun, the hits – but without the cheesiness and the lack of control.

Her last label, deConstruction, had been slowly winding down throughout the 1990s and she was determined that her next move would be the right one. It wasn't just about getting the best deal. It was about finding a place where the people understood and shared her vision of what she should do next. Parlophone, more commonly associated with guitar bands like Radiohead, were the first label to fit the bill.

They promised that not only would she work with some of the finest song-writing talent around, but also that they would provide a marketing budget to match. In the past her labels had been happy to live on the fame she'd accrued from Charlene onwards. Parlophone were prepared to re-launch her as a disco diva, the princess of pop. It was exactly what she'd wanted ever since, a year before on her tour of Australia, she'd at last realised what it was that people loved her for.

She was on stage dressed as a showgirl madly camping it up and she looked out into a sea of happy, smiling faces. The fans had enjoyed her darker, more serious songs, but it was only

Kylie camps it up. *Above:* G.A.Y. at the Astoria, 2000. *Opposite:* Mardi Gras, London, 2000.

when she was playing the role of the glittery pop princess that the crowd really went wild. At that moment her future was clear. From then on, Kylie would let the fans decide which version of her they wanted. At heart she was an entertainer, pure and simple, and that was all she had ever really wanted to be.

In the spring of 2000, she went into the studio with a selection of songs cooked up by the likes of Biff Stanard and Julian Gallagher who'd worked with the Spice Girls. She also worked on two tracks with Guy Chambers and his much more famous writing partner, Robbie Williams. At that time the ex-Take That star had an even higher profile than Kylie. His music, his neuroses and his on-off relationships were never out of the papers. Kylie's record company must have thought that the combination of the two would lift her back into the superleague where she belonged.

As it turned out, that wasn't necessary. Long before their duet 'Kids' came out, Kylie was already back at the top of the charts thanks to her first proper single in more than two years: 'Spinning Around'. "I was so relieved," she said soon afterwards to *B* magazine. "When my manager called me I couldn't take it in. I was playing backgammon at the time and he was teasing me saying: 'Go on, have a guess.' When he told me it was number one I just walked back into the room where all my friends were and started crying."

Usually most of the credit for this success is given to the video. It's true that the image of Kylie dancing on the bar in the legendary gold hot pants is indelibly scored in the memory of millions, but remember that this wasn't the first time she'd used her characteristically cheeky sex appeal in a video. The Barbarella spoof of 'Put Yourself In My Place', where Kylie's clothes mysteriously fall off in space, was much discussed at the time. And don't forget the risque leather look of 'Shocked'.

Above: Kylie and Robbie Williams at an early meeting at the Elle Style Awards in 1997. *Opposite:* A poolside disco with cocktails at the *Light Years* launch party, 2000.

The reason why 'Spinning Around' went to number one was that it was quite simply the catchiest, bounciest, glossiest pop song she'd done for ages. There was more to come on the album, *Light Years*. "I've been much happier doing this album," she said at the time. "I actually can't believe it's done. The whole thing felt like a summer holiday, especially compared to the last album where it was one problem after another."

This time Kylie was going back to the pop that she did best but she was determined to do it her way. As she told *Rolling Stone*, "When I first met the different writers and producers for this one I said, 'These are my keywords: poolside, beach, cocktails and disco.' I wanted to indulge the over-the-top side of my character and I think we did it."

If there's one song that sums up the way Kylie felt during the *Light Years* recording sessions, it's probably 'Your Disco Needs You' – a track that was co-written by Robbie. "Camp doesn't begin to describe that song!" Kylie continued in the same interview. "Camp in capital letters and neon lights still wouldn't do it justice. They had ten male vocalists and they tracked them about three times so on the line where I say 'Kick your ass' you've got 30 beefy vocalists going 'assss!' I think they were slightly embarrassed!"

When [my manager] told me ['Spinning Around'] was number one I just walked back into the room where all my friends were and started crying.

Below and opposite:
Feeling overdressed
compared to her
dancers at the 2000
MTV Awards.

"

When I first met the different writers and producers
for *[Light Years]* I said, 'These are my keywords: poolside,
beach, cocktails and disco.' I wanted to indulge the over-the-
top side of my character and I think we did it.

"

Singing her heart out
at the Hammersmith
Apollo, 2000.

Kylie's umpteenth appearance at the Smash Hits Poll Winners' Party. This time it's the year 2000.

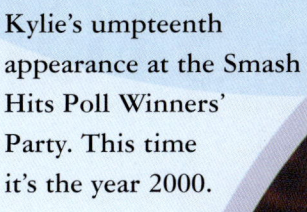

The success of *Light Years* not only restored Kylie to the dizzy heights of her former career, it also made her job fun again. She was working with people who she liked, everyone was pulling in the same direction – in her direction – and the album had a coherence that both the *Kylie Minogue* albums had lacked.

Unfortunately, fame always has a price and it was one that Kylie was well used to by now. The bigger she got, the more outrageous the stories that were printed about her. Occasionally they were hurtful, but most of the time she could just laugh them off. Particularly as very often they had a ridiculous quality that appealed to her well-developed sense of the absurd.

10 OUTRAGEOUS STORIES

1

SHE'S AN ALIEN: At the peak of Kylie's early fame in 1989, a slow news day encouraged *The News Of The World* to decide that Kylie might be from another planet. "The headline was 'Is Kylie An Alien?'" she explained to *Smash Hits*, "and the story was all about how if there was an alien life form on earth then they would have certain features. And they decided to match up these features to mine. They used the topless photo of me on the front page and they were saying that these aliens would have elfin features and small breasts and I think they said big hips, which was a bit rude because I certainly haven't got big hips."

VERDICT: probably untrue

2

SHE'S A DOMINATRIX WITH A FULLY EQUIPPED DUNGEON IN THE BASEMENT OF HER HOUSE: "A friend of mine heard someone saying I had a dungeon," she said to *Vogue*. "People talk about it, saying they've heard it from someone who heard it from someone else, so it must be true. For the record, there is no dungeon," she insists.

VERDICT: firmly denied

3

CUSTOMS OFFICIALS ONCE CONFISCATED A PAIR OF HANDCUFFS FROM HER AT HEATHROW AIRPOT: "That story will follow me around forever," Kylie laughed to *Q* magazine. "Everyone looks at me unconvinced when I explain this. I had this little leather pouch with handcuffs on the handle. I was travelling to Monte Carlo from Heathrow, so I put this small handbag into a larger carrier bag. It never occurred to me that it would be construed as a dangerous item. I put the bag through the X-ray machine and they took them off me. I believe I still have the bag in a drawer somewhere. That one won't be going to Oxfam, I don't quite know what to do with it."

VERDICT: true-ish

4

SHE MADE LOVE TO MICHAEL HUTCHENCE IN THE FIRST-CLASS AREA OF A PLANE WHILE AUSTRALIAN PRIME MINISTER BOB HAWKE WAS SITTING A FEW ROWS IN FRONT: This story was put about by Michael's friend, video director Nick Egan. He even says that Bob Hawke turned around and winked at them. Kylie has never denied that something happened but she says it wasn't quite as it's been pictured. "Let me just say, the guy who told that story wasn't there," she insisted to *Sky* magazine. "They haven't got the facts quite right! But Michael would've told you that story with glee. Probably told it to everybody." Sadly, Bob Hawke has denied seeing anything. "It's absolutely untrue," he said. "The fact is that all my travelling as Prime Minister is done in VIP aircraft – this is just another furphy." (Furphy, by the way, is Australian for rumour.)

VERDICT: inconclusive

5

SHE LOST HER VIRGINITY IN A CUPBOARD: "There are two people who know how I lost my virginity and one of them is not that journalist," she says. "I 'lost it in a cupboard'. That's just spectacular!"

VERDICT: firmly denied

Opposite: Don't believe a word of it. An elfin-faced Kylie, 2000.

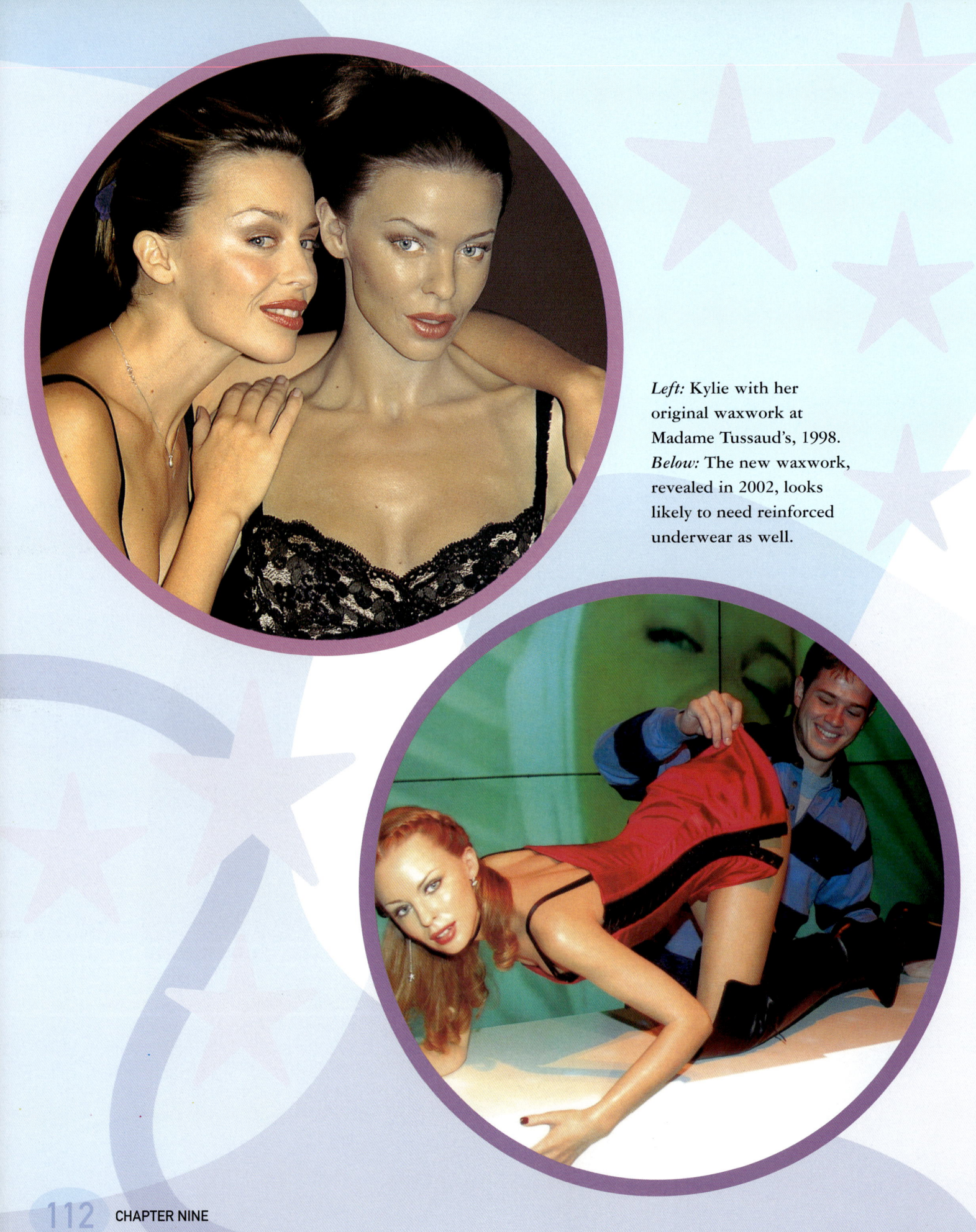

Left: Kylie with her original waxwork at Madame Tussaud's, 1998. *Below:* The new waxwork, revealed in 2002, looks likely to need reinforced underwear as well.

10 OUTRAGEOUS STORIES

THE ORIGINAL WAXWORK OF HER IN MADAM TUSSAUD'S HAD TO BE FITTED WITH EXTRA-STRONG UNDERWEAR TO DEAL WITH ALL THE OVER-EXCITED TOURISTS: According to the *Daily Telegraph*, "Kylie Minogue's sexual magnetism is proving a problem to Madame Tussaud's. Staff have been forced to fit their waxwork model of her with robust underwear, in an effort to reduce the damage being done to the figure by 'gropers'." It's just as well that Kylie's got a sense of humour. "I'm kind of disgusted by it," she said when the story came out, "but have to laugh at the same time."

VERDICT: true

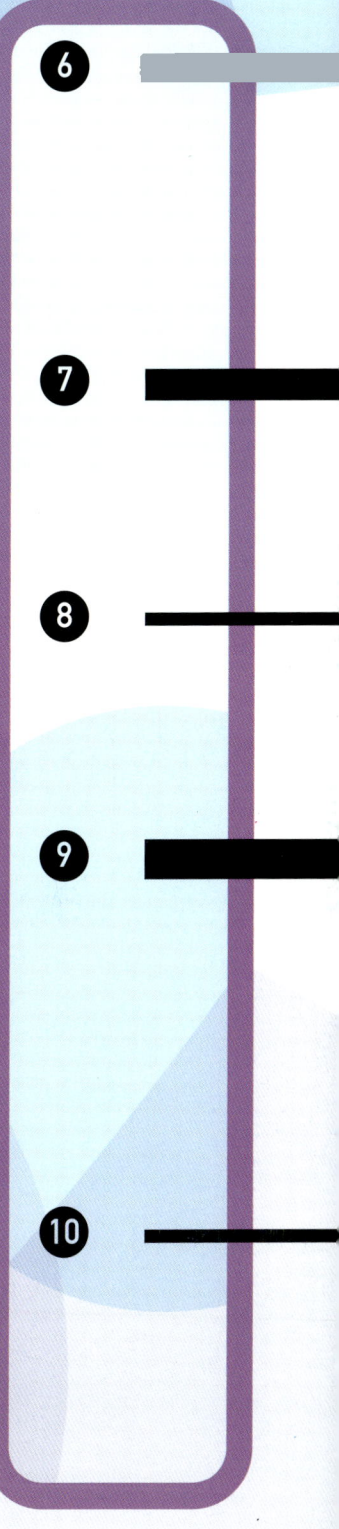

MICHAEL HUTCHENCE TURNED HER INTO A DRUG-CRAZED PARTY ANIMAL: Kylie has admitted that she tried ecstasy when she was with Michael but her behaviour was never quite as extreme as it was painted. "One rumour was that I had been rushed to hospital to get my stomach pumped, when I wasn't even in the country at the time," she said to *Metro*.

VERDICT: untrue

SHE HAS A BOTTOM DOUBLE FOR VIDEOS LIKE SPINNING AROUND: This is a variation on the tired old plastic surgery rumours. Just as some academics like to deny that Shakespeare wrote Shakespeare's plays, some cynical pop critics think that Kylie has a little hired help when it comes to some of her most memorable scenes.

VERDICT: untrue

SHE HAS A TENDENCY TO SLAP PEOPLE WHO PUSH HER TOO FAR: Despite being just a shade over five foot tall and famously easy-going, even Kylie has her limits. Apparently, she once pushed a drag queen up against a wall and held a pool cue to his throat after he kept harassing her and making disparaging comments about her pool skills. More recently, she was alleged to have slapped an American journalist who wrote a feature about her focusing on her supposed "wild times" with Michael Hutchence. The journalist, Bill Schultz, claimed, "In reaction to an interview we did, Kylie Minogue slapped me around the face at a *Saturday Night Live* after-party." However, Kylie's spokesperson insisted, "It was a verbal assault. She told him he needed a slap around the face."

VERDICT: plausible

SHE'S GOING BACK TO NEIGHBOURS: "That," she said to *FHM*, "is the most ridiculous rumour I've heard about myself in ages. I was gobsmacked when I read it. I can only imagine it came from an interview where I jokingly mentioned something like, 'Oh, watch out for me in *Neighbours* in about a year. There'll be a knock at the door and there I'll be.' But I'm really not going back. It wouldn't work. And I don't even know if they'd have me back."

VERDICT: highly unlikely

THE RETURN OF
sex KYLIE: BIGGER THAN EVER

CHAPTER
10
TEN

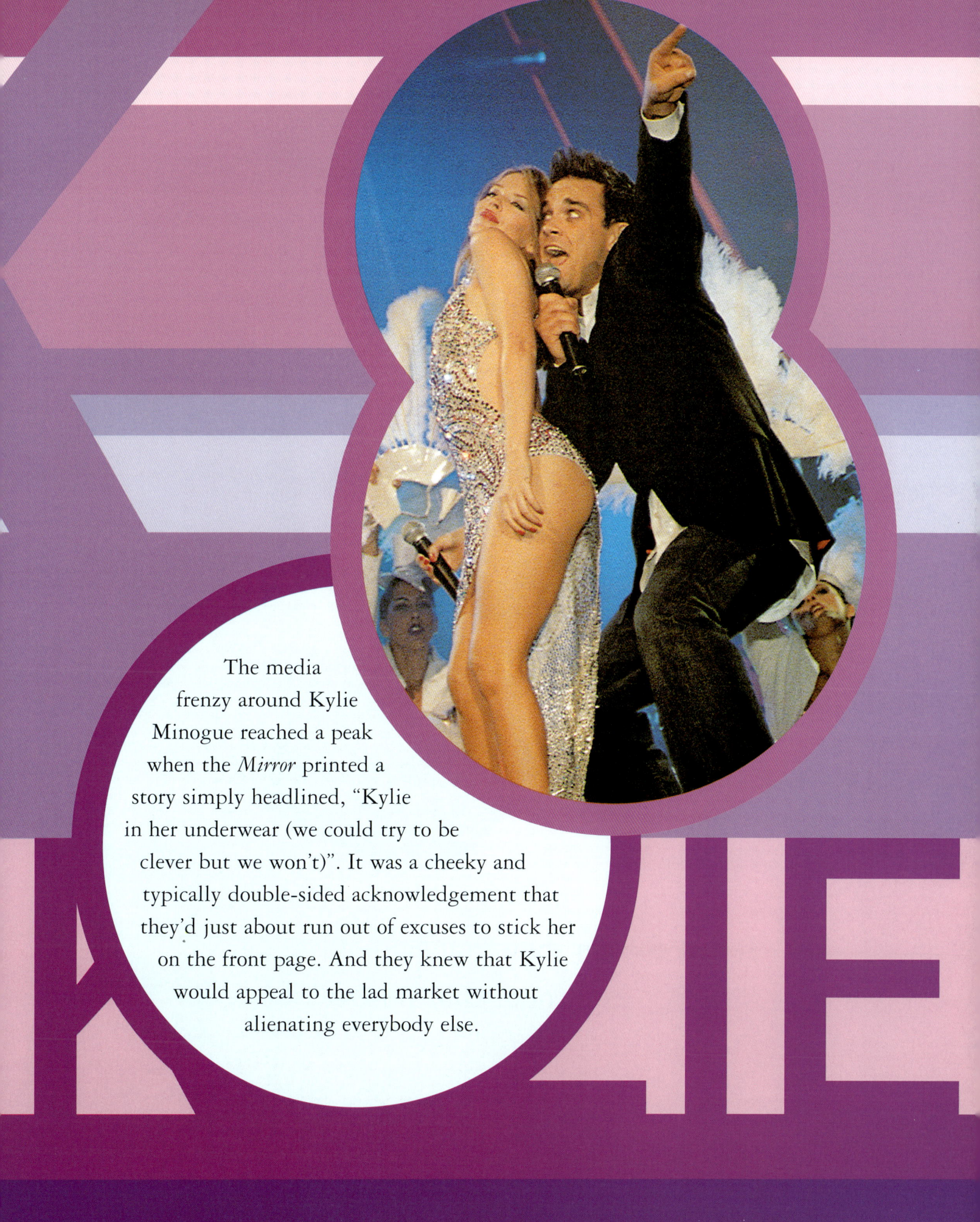

The media frenzy around Kylie Minogue reached a peak when the *Mirror* printed a story simply headlined, "Kylie in her underwear (we could try to be clever but we won't)". It was a cheeky and typically double-sided acknowledgement that they'd just about run out of excuses to stick her on the front page. And they knew that Kylie would appeal to the lad market without alienating everybody else.

"KYLIE"

It just goes to show you cannot relinquish control of your image.

By now Kylie had become a master at slyly mocking her own sex appeal. That's why she could get away with things that might look sleazy from a less shrewd, less wholesome celebrity. "To be honest," she's said "all my so-called sexiness is more like a *Carry On* film. End-of-the-pier fun." And the tabloids loved her for it because they could play the same game, too. Despite being Australian, Kylie is a very British kind of sex symbol.

Her ability to retain an aura of innocence in the most unlikely circumstances was tested to its limits when she starred in the advert for Agent Provocateur lingerie. "I actually stopped breathing when I saw the first edit," she told *The Face*. "I thought, 'I hope my dad's not going to see it.'"

She's always acknowledged that there's a fine line between looking sexy and looking sleazy, but she's never found it difficult to stay on the right side of that line. It's only when others try

and shape her image that you realise how hard the balancing act is.

In summer 2002, Madame Tussaud's announced that they were doing Kylie the honour of making an unprecedented third waxwork of her. She was delighted at the news until she found out that the model showed her on all fours wearing revealing Agent Provocateur underwear.

"They've taken three things I've done," Kylie complained to fansite *LiMBO*. "Yes I've worn that dress, yes I've been photographed in that pose. Yes I've done an Agent Provocateur lingerie ad in those type of knickers. But they've got those three things wrong. The way I work and my team work, I do those three elements in my way. We do them on the right side of taste and in context they work. It's subtlety that will make or break it. It just goes to show you cannot relinquish control of your image."

Above and opposite: **Kylie's latest waxwork. Madame Tussaud's have now lowered the hemline to a more respectable level.**

While Kylie resignedly accepts that if she uses her sex appeal others will use it too, she wasn't prepared for the effect the media hype would have on her love life. In the year 2000, when she was just finishing the *Light Years* album in Los Angeles, she met "a delightful scruff from Essex" called James Gooding. "When I met her," he told London's *Evening Standard* newspaper, "she was just this little, funny, geeky girl who I thought was really cute."

Despite the fact that he was eight years younger, they immediately hit it off. To begin with there was no pressure and that was the way they both liked it. "I've never called James 'Mr Right'," said Kylie. "It's been blown out of all proportion." He may not have been the love of her life but she was still happier than she'd been for a long time. "I've been very happy in my personal life and that reflects in what I do," she told *New Woman* when asked where the new, happy vibe of *Light Years* came from. "For a long time I spent nights alone, not crying but wondering what was going on with my love life. It was hard because when I went out with someone, the media would link me in with them emotionally. That wasn't the case as often I'd return to my empty place on my own."

MTV Awards, 2000.

CHAPTER TEN

Their relationship even survived the attentions of the notoriously flirtatious Robbie Williams. Robbie had first met her as a star-struck teenager in the early days of his career in boy band Take That. By the time they collaborated on 'Kids' and 'Your Disco Needs You', though, the callow youth had grown up into a self-confident, if confused, pop star in his own right.

An affair between the two stars would have been a publicist's dream and the tabloids desperately wanted to believe that something was going on, but Kylie and Robbie dashed their hopes. "I had a boyfriend through all of that," she explained to *More* magazine. "I think we both know how to play up to the camera and that really was all there was to it. There was definitely a chemistry when we were working but beyond that … He's a good guy, who makes me laugh."

Kylie wasn't averse to using her legendary allure to unsettle the cheeky star. She appeared on stage with him in Manchester and, although they'd been chatting happily an hour or so before, he wasn't prepared for her appearance as she sashayed towards him. "It was just priceless because Rob's so in control on stage, he's almost impossible to rattle," she laughed to *GQ*. "But he hadn't seen the dress I was going to wear – it was the little silver slip of a thing which I wore at the MTV awards too. His face was absolutely beautiful because for a second he completely lost it. All the super-confidence was suddenly stripped away and he was like, 'Unnghh!' It was excellent. As soon as I was out of sight he was back in control but just for a minute there he was sweating. I loved it."

However, as she said, she had a boyfriend through all of that, so nothing was going to happen between the two stars. Things were changing for James and Kylie, though. He'd met her before 'Spinning Around' had

The dress that blew
Robbie Williams' cool at
the MTV Awards.

reestablished her as Britain's favourite sex symbol. Even then, there was still tremendous interest from the press in what she was up to but it wasn't anything like the obsessive interest she was now starting to attract.

As Kylie's success grew and grew at the beginning of the third millennium, her work schedule began to resemble the gruelling regime she'd endured in the early days of her career. Inevitably, her relationship with James suffered. Although he could accept how important her work was to her, the intense criticism and scrutiny of the press was something else. To begin with the media interest mostly focused on rumours that James had had posters of her on his wall when he was a boy. "None of it's true!" Kylie insisted. "Like he would have a poster of me! Obviously, you don't know him," she said to *Sky* magazine, "but it's absolutely preposterous! I don't want to perpetuate that anymore. That's so embarrassing for him and it's not true."

More seriously, every time James spoke to another woman the newspapers would be full of reports of his supposed infidelity. After a time it got too much. Just seven minutes before she was due to go on stage in Manchester, she made an emotional phone call to *The Sun*'s showbiz desk to try to set things straight.

"I am devastated,'" Kylie apparently told the paper. "There have been a lot of tears, particularly today, and I've only just felt strong enough to talk about it. I'm numb. I cannot imagine him not being a part of my life. It's been a real emotional rollercoaster. I've felt sick all day."

"I feel I've been the one who's been selfish," she continued. "There hasn't been any kind of confrontation between us. My career in the last year has just exploded and what has happened is I've become so dedicated to that. It's very hard being Kylie," she finished sadly. "Perhaps it's even harder being Kylie's boyfriend."

It was very clear from this that Kylie didn't really want to finish with James. Just as when she'd split up from Michael Hutchence, it seemed as though she'd somehow broken up with him without quite meaning to. "I keep having that song going through my head, 'Breaking Up Is Hard To Do'," she told *Marie Claire*. "Us breaking up is nothing to do with our feelings for each other – I would say that a lot of it is media-related pressure. Take that out of the equation and we'd probably be fine."

"Relationships are fraught with difficulties," Kylie had said long before. "Even when it's wonderful, there's always something around the corner to test the partnership." As it turned out, that something was a new level of success that even she had never experienced before. If her love life was to be reignited, she needed to negotiate that first.

> "My career in the last year has just exploded and what has happened is I've become so dedicated to that. It's very hard being Kylie. Perhaps it's even harder being Kylie's boyfriend.

FEVER

FEVER

KYLIE

CHAPTER

1

ELEVEN

Just as in her Stock, Aitken and Waterman days, Kylie didn't wait for long after the success of *Light Years* before going back in the studio again. Kylie knows that success can be fleeting and she wanted to capitalise on the high profile she'd achieved in 2001. So, at the end of the year, she began work on her seventh album, *Fever*.

It's not easy being green…

Above: Singing with Kermit on the TV show *An Audience With Kylie Minogue*, 2001.

Opposite: At the US premiere of *Moulin Rouge*, in which she played the green Absinthe Fairy.

If the buzzwords for *Light Years* had been "poolside, beach, cocktails and disco", then this time maybe you could add "limousines, sex, clubs and glamour". *Fever* retained the same pop sensibility as its predecessor but it was an altogether cooler album with less of the self-conscious, self-mocking air of kitsch. For once there was no need for a relaunch. Instead there was more of a seamless transition from one style to another.

However, even if she'd taken ten years off, 'Can't Get You Out Of My Head' would have put her right back to the top of the tree. "I fell in love with it the first time I heard the demo,"

Kylie told *More*. "Cathy Dennis and Rob Davis wrote it especially for me, I was so excited. I was like: 'When can we do it? I'll do it today.'"

As ever, Kylie's instincts were spot on. 'Can't Get You Out Of My Head' would eventually go to number one in 23 countries. Incredibly, after all those years, after all the success she'd had in the 1980s and 1990s, her biggest-selling single ever would be her 33rd: a song penned by a fleetingly famous singer and the guitarist from 1970s glam-rockers Mud.

Cathy Dennis and Rob Davis could hardly be less alike but in a strange way they both had some understanding of Kylie's life. Cathy had

KYLIE

'I fell in love with ['Can't Get You Out Of My Head'] the first time I heard the demo. Cathy Dennis and Rob Davis wrote it especially for me, I was so excited. I was like: 'When can we do it? I'll do it today.''

been successful for a short time in the 1990s and, although she'd done reasonably well in America, she found the hassles of stardom too much to take. She was particularly averse to the pressure on young female singers to wear as few clothes as possible. To be able to concentrate on writing and leave everything else to a natural performer, exhibitionist and flirt like Kylie must have been a joy.

Rob Davis had written songs for Mud when he was young, but in the 1970s it was strictly understood that legendary production team Nicky Chinn and Mike Chapman wrote the singles: catchy, somewhat cheesy numbers like Mud's 'Tiger Feet'. In a way, Chinn and Chapman were a precursor of Stock, Aitken and Waterman, so Rob understood the uncomfortable experience of knowing that somebody else was pulling the strings.

Perhaps it was the mutual understanding between the three that made 'Can't Get You Out Of My Head' the triumph that it is. Cathy brought the lyrics and a bright, breezy pop sensibility, Rob brought the dancefloor credibility that he'd picked up working with the likes of Spiller, and Kylie brought her own magical, effervescent Kylieness.

Even when the song was cut, nobody was sure that it would go to the top of the charts in the UK. There was still one major obstacle. During the 1990s, when Kylie had been experimenting with her image and her music, a new face had emerged as the personification of pop – or rather, this time, it was five faces: The Spice Girls.

Four of the five girls had already released solo singles and they'd all been massive hits. Now it was to be the turn of the most famous Spice Girl of them all: Victoria Beckham, aka Posh Spice. By complete coincidence Kylie's 'Can't Get You Out Of My Head' was to be released on the same day as Victoria's solo debut 'Not Such An Innocent Girl'.

Performing in Glasgow during her *On A Night Like This* tour, 2001.

"I rang my manager as soon as I heard," Kylie told *Heat* magazine, "and asked whether we should change the date but it would have been a nightmare. Also, I'd just be up against someone else. The cards had been dealt and I just thought I should play the game and go along with it."

There was nothing else she could do. She may have thought the idea of music as a competitive sport was slightly ridiculous but, to begin with, the papers had a field day – Spice Girl bashing had become something of a sport of its own. As the sales figures started to come through, it became clear that the purported competition wasn't even close. Kylie was number one by a mile and Victoria was several places behind.

Although the battle ended up as a complete non-event, Kylie still felt bad for her supposed rival and, before the chart was announced, she sent Victoria a message of support. "I sent a note because it was getting crazy and I just felt it was human courtesy," she continued to *Heat*. "I just said, 'Supposedly, we're at war but it's not like that: there's not any ill feeling.'"

Kylie woos America at the MTV Awards, 2000.

"It's very hard for me to convey what [performing at the Sydney Olympics] was like. I felt like I was in the middle of some weird special effect where you're dragged into another dimension … It was perfect. The whole stadium was dazzling!

Right and below: Opening ceremony of the 2000 Sydney Paralympics.

Kylie had experienced cruel, personal criticism herself and she knew how it felt to have the media against you, but she'd discovered that the best answer to that was to be successful. Her personal life may have been suffering but in her career she seemed to scale new heights every week. Perhaps the greatest of these was her entirely unexpected breakthrough in America.

The seeds of her success were planted back in 2000 with an unforgettable appearance at the spectacular closing ceremony of the Sydney Olympic games. A worldwide TV audience numbering in the billions saw her carried into the stadium on a surfboard by burly Australian footballers.

"It's very hard for me to convey what it was like," she enthused to *B* magazine. "I felt like I was in the middle of some weird special effect where you're dragged into another dimension. There were drag queens everywhere, prawns on bicycles, Elle MacPherson walking out on this massive camera lens … it was perfect. The whole stadium was dazzling!"

Dressed as a showgirl with long feathers extending from her head, Kylie sang Abba's 'Dancing Queen' and then her own 'On A Night Like This'. It was an impressive finale for what had been a hugely successful games for Sydney and Australia. Even America was forced to sit up and take notice.

However, by the time 'Can't Get You Out Of My Head' came out, all that was forgotten. In the States there are two main ways for a song to become a hit: either it's picked up by the hundreds of local radio stations, or it's picked up by the mighty MTV. In the past, both had always thought that Kylie was too frothy, too ephemeral for the American market, where even pop stars have to take themselves seriously – or at least pretend to. This time, though, MTV liked what they saw. The famous video for 'Can't Get You Out Of My Head'

Smash Hits Poll
Winners Party, 2001.

was soon a favourite of the network and Kylie was assured of her first hit in the States since 'The Loco-motion' way back in 1987.

She was still a little apprehensive about having to go through the gruelling process of feeding the massive, disparate American media. At least in the rest of the world everybody knew who she was. "The thought of having to explain how you say my name and tell my soap opera beginnings again and again to mid-western stations is more than I can bear," she told *The Face* ruefully.

Assistance on the promotional front came from an unexpected source, though. At the MTV awards her old heroine and fellow pop survivor Madonna arrived wearing a T-shirt with the words "Kylie Minogue" proudly emblazoned across the front. "To see my name on her T-shirt was surreal," a somewhat bemused but flattered Kylie told *More*. "It was great. The first thing I think I said was: 'Hi! Nice to meet you.' She asked me if I liked the T-shirt and I said: 'Yes, I do like the T-shirt, thank you.' The whole thing just had her savvy. But I did appreciate the sign of solidarity."

At that point Kylie was probably as big as it was possible to get outside of America. The next singles from *Fever* – 'In Your Eyes' and 'Love At First Sight' – were ubiquitous across the airwaves and she dominated the front pages of the tabloids like no other star. Luckily for them, there was a plentiful stream of fresh stories as *Fever: The Tour* began to wind its way around the globe.

Above: Madonna shows pop star solidarity at the MTV awards, 2000.
Opposite: Kylie checks out Madonna's show in Brixton, 2000.

FEVER on THE ROAD

KYLIE

CHAPTER 12 TWELVE

Throughout her career, a Kylie tour has always been a big deal. To begin with there was the fascination of seeing whether the tiny Australian could actually sing or whether she was just Rick Astley speeded up. Then, after those rumours were crushed, the speculation turned to the nature of her costumes, to SexKylie, controversy and drama. The question was, would the *Fever* tour bring any new surprises?

By the time the *Fever* tour came around, everybody knew that Kylie could sing and there was very little mileage left in controversy. Her management and stylists knew that it would be incredibly difficult to surprise people this time. Nevertheless, they were determined to try.

Fever began in Cardiff, Wales, on 26 April 2002 and it ended a staggering 51 dates later in her home town of Melbourne, Australia, on 16 August. There were to be seven stage acts, elaborate costumes made by Dolce and Gabbana and Agent Provocateur, and a permanent crew of over a hundred people. It was estimated to have cost more than £2.5 million.

Where her previous year's *On A Night Like This* tour was about pure fun, re-establishing her as the princess of pop, *Fever* would be a much more sophisticated and glamorous affair. Although her designers, management and record company had planned everything down to the last detail, however, they couldn't have prevented the one problem that afflicts global superstars just as it does karaoke singers or pub rock crooners.

RoboKylie on the first date of the *Fever* tour.

Just days before the opening date, Kylie lost her voice. It was a cruel blow after she'd worked so hard to show people that she could sing. She was reported to have tried vocal exercises, Chinese herbs, homeopathic remedies and throat massage, anything in a desperate attempt to be ready for her first show, but right up until the time she was supposed to be on stage, she still felt hoarse and unwell.

In the Cardiff International Arena, the 10,000-plus crowd shuffled anxiously as the announced time for her to appear came and went. Then, suddenly, 'The Sound Of Music' began yodelling out of the speakers and there was a huge roar from the fans as Kylie emerged, mouthing the Julie Andrews classic, wearing a shiny silver space suit. Gradually she began to disrobe, casting aside her metallic shell and emerging in a sparkly silver top and mini-skirt as she segued seamlessly from 'The Sound Of Music' into 'Come Into My World' from the *Fever* album.

The roar subsided to an intrigued hum. It was already clear Kylie had moved on from the simple pop stylings of 'A Night Like This'. The *Fever* tour would take in influences ranging from the violent film classic *A Clockwork Orange* to *Carry On* films and *Star Trek*.

"It's quite brave in places," Kylie admitted to Australia's *Herald Sun*. "It takes about three songs before you get what you think you're going to get. Last time people went crazy through the whole show. This time, you see people just watching me, and I start wondering, 'Do they like it?' – but they're just taking it all in."

It might have been a departure but, like the album, the *Fever* tour was a huge commercial and critical success. It became the fastest-selling tour in UK history, beating Madonna's *Drowned World* tour of the previous year. Critics in the UK were almost unanimous in their praise. "Phenomenally staged, flawlessly performed

and bursting with enough pop cultural references to make an Eminem video look like *The Antiques Roadshow*," gushed the *NME*, and they weren't alone.

The set reached right back through her history, turning 'I Should Be So Lucky' into a trance odyssey, seamlessly segueing tracks together and finishing with the bootleg mix of 'Can't Get You Out Of My Head' and New Order's 'Blue Monday' that she'd premiered at the Brit Awards.

It wasn't until the tour reached Australia that the show encountered some criticism. One review implied that she might not have been singing and Kylie was uncharacteristically furious. "That completely infuriated me within half a second," she raged to the *Herald Sun*. "I have never mimed; come up with something new. It's boring and so stupid. That kind of snide comment is the same thing I have had to battle against from day one."

The reaction of her hometown fans in Melbourne made up for any lazy criticisms. Australians have often bemoaned their national tendency towards "tall poppy syndrome", where people feel the need to cut the successful down to size, and for many years Kylie had more criticism at home than anywhere else. Here, though, was clear evidence that she was massively loved by the Australian public.

Kylie strikes a pose, *Fever* tour, 2002.

"I do love being home,"
she continued to the *Herald Sun*.
"The Melbourne audiences have been just
sensational. This is the last week, and I know
by the final show on Friday, I'll be completely
emotional. I'll be in floods of tears on stage. I was
a bit weepy during the first show on Saturday
night. I just had all these thoughts flashing
through my mind of high school, where I grew
up, how supportive people have been – and
it all got a bit emotional."

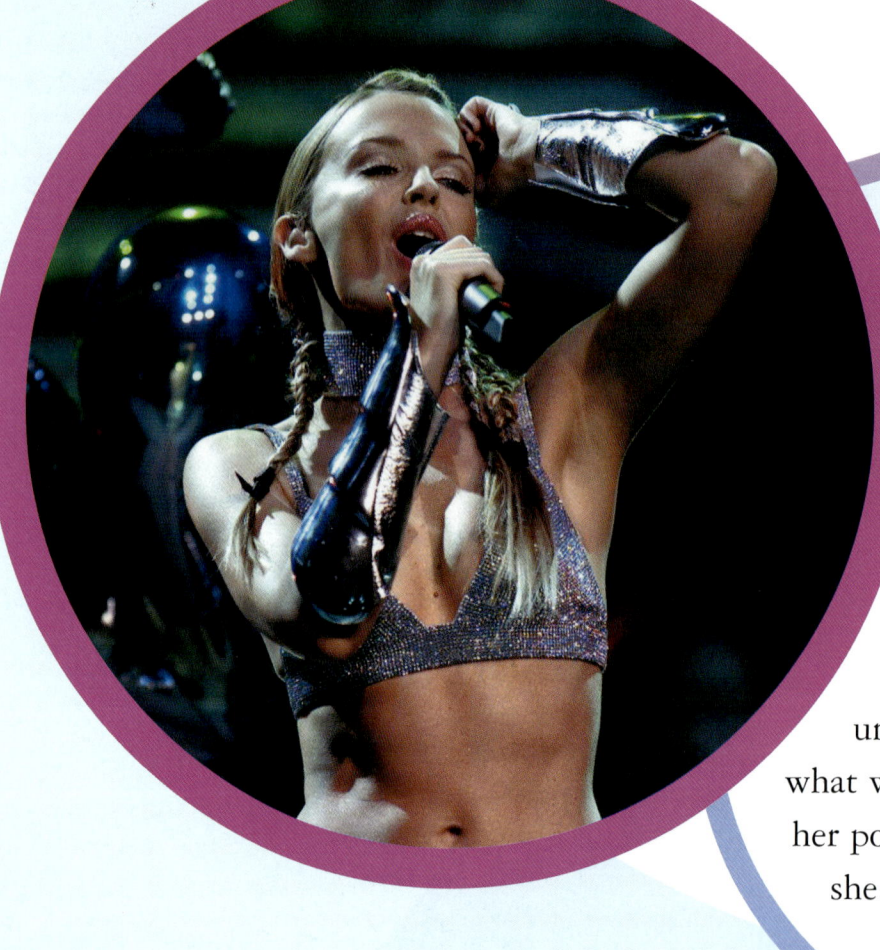

As a thank you
she added one extra,
unscheduled song to the
set list: 'Koocachoo'. While
her dancers milled around
uncertainly, not quite knowing
what was happening, she revelled in
her popularity. Even after 51 dates
she wasn't quite ready for the
Fever tour to end.

Performing 'Can't Get Blue Monday Out of My Head' at the Brits, 2002.

THE FEVER TOUR SET LIST

Intro: The Sound Of Music

Come Into My World

Shocked

Love At First Sight

Fever

Spinning Around

Where Is The Feeling?/The Crying Game/
Put Yourself In My Place/Finer
Feelings/Dangerous Game/The Crying Game

Confide In Me

Cowboy Style/Double Dutch

Kids

Intro/On A Night Like This

The LocoMotion

In Your Eyes/Please Stay/Rhythm Of The
Night/Rhythm Is Gonna Get You/In Your Eyes

Limbo

Light Years/I Feel Love/Light Years

I Should Be So Lucky/Dreams

Encore:

Burning Up

Better The Devil You Know

Can't Get Blue Monday Out Of My Head

LIFE AFTER FEVER

13

CHAPTER THIRTEEN

LIFE AFTER FEVER

Kylie had barely come off tour when there was a flurry of fresh announcements and rumours. The first, and perhaps the most predictable, was that she was considering taking time off to start a family with James Gooding. The two had got back together barely a month after they'd split up and they were said to be, in the usual cliché, inseparable.

Kylie and James –
"inseparable".

"

James is the only man she wants to have babies with and Kylie is aware that if she does not take time off for him she will lose her chance.

"

According to anonymous informants in London's *Evening Standard*, "the split really shook Kylie up and she has decided to put her career on hold for a little bit to give her personal life a chance. She knows that if she wants children she has to start thinking about it now. James is the only man she wants to have babies with and Kylie is aware that if she does not take time off for him she will lose her chance."

Given that Kylie had been travelling around the world for most of the last four months, and appearing on stage more nights than not, it's hard to see how they can have been "inseparable", but it's not at all hard to see why such a prospect must have appealed to the exhausted star.

"I've been used to recognition and fame for years now, but the last three months it just seems like I'm not sure what's happening because of the success," she said to *The Face* recently. "It is making me question what I need in my life. I just need more time for me, for a start. Then I need time for my friends, for my boyfriend, for my family. But I don't even have any for me at the moment. I'm hardly ever on my own. And the one thing that frightens me the most is loneliness. I've got to face up to myself at some point. Work's easy. Life's hard."

Even when she split up with Stephane Sednaoui, Kylie told reporters: "I loved being in love because it's the one thing in life that you can't control." Throughout those nights of living out of a suitcase on the *Fever* tour, she must have dreamed of settling down, but although Kylie has never seemed particularly driven, there's always another project waiting around the corner, another excuse to get back to work.

The first and most significant story to come out in the weeks following the tour was the news that Madonna had written a track for her. The song 'Alone Again' was swiftly recorded and in August there were suggestions that it would be a double A-side with 'Come Into My World' from *Fever*. "I don't think she's ever given a song of hers to another artist," Kylie said excitedly. "It's quite rare."

To make things even more exciting, and to give gossip columnists palpitations, the single was originally scheduled for 21 October – the same day as her sister Dannii's comeback single 'Put The Needle On The Record'. Perhaps remembering the stress of the Kylie vs Posh Spice battle, Dannii's track came forward to 7 October and Kylie's went back to November.

"I've heard a few songs from Dannii's album and they're great," Kylie enthused to the *Herald Sun*. "I've just been bigging her up all over the place. I love her new single, I can't get it out of my head! I had to text her. She's earned some success and joy, I'm thrilled. And our singles won't be out at the same time – I'm sure the papers would love to have some war between us, but it won't happen."

At the same time there were also rumours that she was to record a duet with ex-Eternal star Louise. These were fairly quickly quashed. Kylie would be too busy collaborating on a new coffee table book with her stylist Will Baker, to be called *La La La*, promoting her latest range of LoveKylie lingerie and, of course, performing the new single.

Above and opposite:
Kylie puts her troubles behind her at the 2002 San Remo Festival.

Then there were rumours that she might duet with Australian actress Nicole Kidman, whom she'd appeared alongside in *Moulin Rouge*. Despite the fact that nothing formal has been arranged, Kylie has said that it's something she would definitely like to do in the future if the two stars have time. That, though, is a big if.

Nevertheless Kylie does have her own plans to start spreading the spirit of girl-power solidarity and this is where the possibilities get really intriguing. In 2002 she wrote a song for girl band Atomic Kitten called 'Feels So Good'. Understandably they were ecstatic. "Oh my god! I went crazy," says Natasha Hamilton of the group. "I've grown up with Kylie. She is a big inspiration to me."

It was a huge coup for Atomic Kitten. They had recently sacked the songwriters who created them, Andy McCluskey (formerly of 1980s synth band OMD) and his writing partner Stuart Kershaw. The girls claimed that they were only being paid 4p for each single that they sold and that they'd expected more when they became successful. With Kylie's support it seemed that the Pop Puppets Liberation Front was on the march.

If the Atomic Kitten single does well, it opens up another possibility for Kylie. She's always wanted to have more songwriting input on her own albums but the modern music

> "A 17-year-old today is a lot more savvy than when I was that age … I do find it quite astonishing that I'm still here, doing it. And I've done so much since I was 18, which is how old those girls are now. It's a whole lifetime."

Left: On her way to the 2002 Capital Radio Awards. *Opposite:* Clutching her Brits.

With James Gooding at the NRJ Music Awards, 2002.

industry doesn't like pop acts writing their own songs. For solo artists to write and record an album on their own would take, at the very least, a year. And to "work" that album – ie, promote it around the world – would take at least another year, but record companies expect their artists to produce and promote a new record every 12 months.

The maths doesn't add up even for a workaholic like Kylie. As Rob Davis, who co-wrote 'Can't Get You Out Of My Head', put it in an interview with the *Guardian*: "Even if you're a genius like George Michael, it takes him two years to make an album, but pop artists like Kylie Minogue need the killer songs every year. They have to do interviews all day, it's really time-consuming, and writing and production is a full-time job. They can't just go away and spend ages making an album. Kylie went away for a couple of years and everybody thought she'd had it."

Kylie is now 34 and she may not want to spend her life as a pop idol forever. She may have seen off dozens of competitors, from the likes of Sinitta and Bananarama in the 1980s to Britney Spears and Christina Aguilera more recently, but there are always new artists coming through. "A 17-year-old today is a lot more savvy than when I was that age," she's said. "I am in competition with them, but then I'm competing with everyone. I do find it quite astonishing that I'm still here, doing it. And I've done so much since I was 18, which is how old those girls are now. It's a whole lifetime."

So, could Kylie fly away to a remote island with James Gooding and write songs for other artists every now and then? Could she stand people thinking that she'd "had it"? It's a possibility that might alarm many of her fans. Although she's always said that performing is the part of her "job" that she enjoys the most, after 15 years nobody would begrudge her at least a bit of a rest.

Kylie thinks about more shelf space – the 2002 Monte Carlo Awards.

At the height of *Fever* fever, she said something that she could have said any time in the last 15 years: "This thing that's happening at the moment is just temporary. Everyone's just a little overexcited and I know it will pass."

However, for 15 years it hasn't passed. Even during the slowest periods of her career, she's still been a huge star. For 15 years she's tried to cram the life of a pop star, actress, songwriter and businesswoman into that delicate five foot one frame. It hasn't left much room for herself and maybe one day she will decide to disappear to have babies or to write – but nobody would bet against her coming back and topping the charts again in another 15 years.

Kylie might need a new house for all her awards! *Left:* NME Awards, 2002. *Opposite:* MTV Awards, New York, August 2002.

PHOTOGRAPHIC CREDITS

The publishers would like to thank the following sources for their kind permission to reproduce the pictures in this book:

All Action: 17; /Olly Hewitt: 76; /Dave Hogan: 49, 104; /J.K.: 2tr, 132–133; /Suzan Moore: 112t, 126, 142; /Ellis O'Brien: 77; /Duncan Raban: 29, 36, 44, 58, 61, 62, 63, 69, 91; /Justin Thomas: 3tr, 72cr, 75, 153.

Corbis: 141; /Rune Hellestad: 109; /John Marshall: 1; /Neal Preston: 51; /Andy Willsher: 107.

Famous: /Peter Aitchison: 102; /Fred Duval: 7, 10, 84b, 95; /Bob Foy: 130; /Pauline French: 129; /Marc Gilliam: 125, 137; /Rob Howard: 37, 92; /Pat Lyttle: 47; /Jeff Walker: 85, 150.

Getty Images: /Anthony Harvey: 155; /Jamie Squire: 134t.

Redferns: /Kieran Doherty: 72b; /Glenn A. Baker Archive: 84t; /Tim Hall: 34; /Mick Hutson: 60, 98; /JM International: 87, 143, 154; /Bob King: 53, 56; /Martin Philbey: 88–89; /S & G: 33; /Jim Sharpe: 2tl, 144.

Rex Features: 3tl, 14, 15, 20, 21, 24, 26, 31, 38, 43, 48br, 52, 55, 94, 101, 136, 157; /Austral International: 39; /Brendan Beirne: 28; /Chris Bergman: 111; /Mel Bouzad: 79; /Mauro Carraro: 23; /Peter Carrette: 134b; /Neil Genower: 35; /Glories: 64; /Dave Hogan: 40, 41; /Edward Hurst: 71; /Nils Jorgensen: 112b, 116, 117, 118–119, 158; /Tony Kyriacou: 121; /Ken McKay: 128; /Andrew Milligan: 145;

/Camila Morandi: 152; /Andrew Murray: 59; /Nikos: 103; /Erik C. Pendzich: 159; /Doug Peters: 122; /Profile Press: 68; /Brian Rasic: 46, 50, 74, 108, 115, 123, 135, 139, 146–147; /Robert Rosen: 45, 48l; /Rotex: 13; /Sipa Press: 4–5, 82, 156; /Sipa Press/Niviere/DPPI: 89; /Charles Sykes: 9, 160; /Richard Young: 18, 57, 65, 72tl, 97, 99br, 99tl, 105, 149.

S.I.N.: /Antony Medley: 70; /Tony Mott: 67, 73; /Andy Willsher: 6, 81, 106.

Every effort has been made to acknowledge correctly and contact the source and/or copyright holder of each picture, and Carlton Publishing Group apologises for any unintentional errors or omissions, which will be corrected in future editions of this book.